CYCLING
YORKSHIRE

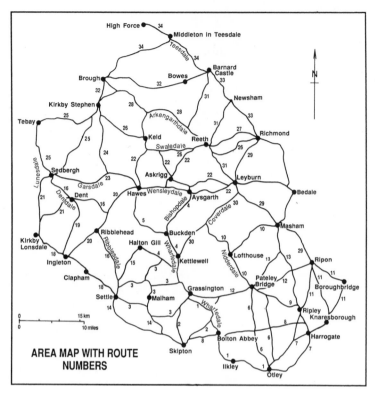

AREA MAP WITH ROUTE NUMBERS

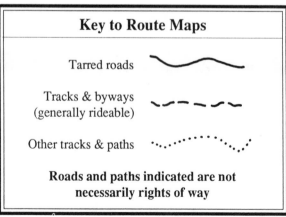

Key to Route Maps

Tarred roads

Tracks & byways
(generally rideable)

Other tracks & paths

**Roads and paths indicated are not
necessarily rights of way**

CYCLING
in the
YORKSHIRE
DALES

MPC

Published by:
Moorland Publishing Co Ltd,
Moor Farm Road,
Airfield Estate,
Ashbourne,
Derbyshire DE6 1HD
England

British Library Cataloguing in Publi-
cation Data
Harries, Richard
    Cycling in the Yorkshire Dales.
    1. North Yorkshire. National Parks.
Yorkshire Dales
    National Park - Visitor's guides
    I. Title
    914.28'404858

    ISBN 0 86190 330 7

Black & White origination by:
Monochrome Scanning Ltd
Printed in the UK by:
Richard Clay Ltd, Bungay, Suffolk

Cover picture: The Fleet Moss road
near Oughtershaw (F. Moore).

Photographs have been supplied as
follows:
R. Harries: pp 22, 24, 42, 71, 82,
85, 97, 111, 118, 131, 140, 145,
151, 164, 167, 175, 179; F. Moore:
p28; MPC Picture Collection: pp
20, 31, 35, 37, 41, 45, 47, 127, 153,
155, 161, 183.

The Author
Richard Harries is a chartered Civil
Engineer specialising in transport
planning. Apart from cycling his
hobbies include walking, collecting
old maps and guidebooks, and
playing the classical guitar. He is
married with a young daughter.
    This is his second book,
following *Cycling in the Lake
District*, published by MPC in 1984.

CONTENTS

FOREWORD

In recent years there has been a resurgence in the popularity of cycling. This has been partly due to the development of the 'mountain bike', a cycle suited to a much wider choice of terrain than that favoured by the traditional touring cyclist.

The Yorkshire Dales is a region ideally suited to exploration by all kinds of cycle and in his book, *Cycling in the Yorkshire Dales*, Richard Harries has put together a number of routes which cover the Yorkshire Dales National Park and much of the surrounding area.

The routes are based mainly on minor roads but included are many options to cycle on Yorkshire's 'green' or unmetalled roads. These provide excellent tracks for the mountain bike rider or 'rough-stuff' tourer. These tracks, inaccessible to cars and often too remote for walkers, offer the opportunity to explore the Dales away from the crowds.

Cycling in the Yorkshire Dales features much information not found in guides written for motorists or walkers — route and tour planning, distances, time schedules and an indication of severity of routes. In addition there are details of cycle hire, rights of way and descriptions of the area covered by the routes and the attractions to be seen along the way. As cycling continues to grow then we will need books to help enjoy our sport away from today's crowded main roads. *Cycling in the Yorkshire Dales* offers this help in one handy-sized attractive book.

INTRODUCTION

The area covered by this book comprises the whole of the Yorkshire Dales National Park and the immediate approaches, being bounded in the east more or less by the A1 Great North Road, to the south and south-west by the Leeds—Skipton—Kendal road, to the west by the River Lune and to the north by the A66 from Scotch Corner to Brough. While considerable tracts have been made open to the public as 'access land' (subject to certain restrictions) elsewhere access is limited to public roads and other rights of way. Similarly although the National Trust own large areas of land in the Dales much of this is tenanted farmland with no special rights of public access. Outside the National Park, and separated from it by a tract of less interesting scenery, lies Teesdale which is rightfully awarded coverage. This area strays beyond the present boundaries of Yorkshire into Cumbria and County Durham, but much of it formerly lay within the North Riding of Yorkshire.

Virtually all the roads in the Yorkshire Dales are covered in this book by a number of routes linking obvious centres and places of interest. For each route an introduction is given, which briefly describes what there is to see on the way, whether the road is difficult or not for cycling, suggested detours and any alternative routes that might be considered. A detailed description then follows, giving directions where necessary, warnings of dangerous hills, points of interest which might otherwise be missed and background information. Intersecting routes are cross-referenced, so prolonged tours or round trips can be devised with ease. Although the descriptions are, of course, for cyclists travelling in one particular direction those heading the 'wrong' way have not been forgotten and any salient points have been covered.

The area is excellent for cycling and within its bounds there are no large centres of population. The district is not dissected by any major traffic route so the roads are almost without exception lightly trafficked and the cyclist need not shy away even from main roads. The area is of course hilly, but if one plans accordingly and accepts that the scenery is to be enjoyed and not rushed through, then this need not detract from the pleasures of cycletouring. For example, even crossing a major pass such as the 'Buttertubs' will only take the cyclist an hour or so, travelling from Wensleydale to Swaledale providing a whole new world of exploration. In fact the more demanding inter-valley crossings can generally be avoided with careful planning and the dale bottoms themselves provide some of the most enjoyable cycling runs in Britain.

Most of the scenic attractions and local beauty spots are within easy walking distance of a road or track, so even the backpacking hiker has no advantage over the light-travelling cycle rider. It is arguable that the cyclist has more scope for getting away from crowds than the walker: solitude is not to be found on top of Ingleborough or Simon's Seat but on the Stake Road, or lonely moorland exits from Nidderdale — tracks so remote that they are the preserve of the rough-stuff cyclist.

One advantage of touring by bike is independence of other forms of transport. To travel under one's own steam is satisfying in itself, but anyone who has visited places such as Malham or Grassington and seen the mayhem caused by parked and moving cars will be thankful not to be part of it. Using bus services to tour the Dales is impossible — even getting to the remoter dales is difficult and inter-valley routes are practically non-existent.

Great care has been taken with the provision of distances which are shown at the start of each route and under the descriptions of major centres. Distances to places not on the direct route are given in parentheses. In calculating travel times a rule of thumb would then be to allow 12 to 15mph on the flat, counting each 50m rise as an extra mile. In a hilly area it is often difficult to estimate how long it will take between places, but with this book a day's ride can be accurately planned in advance. For bridleway and similar routes, journey times are quoted wherever possible. These are all based on the author's experience and, as they exclude intermediate stops, are best taken as minima for planning purposes.

Maps

The maps given for each route have been drawn specifically for this book and taken together form a complete cycling atlas of the Yorkshire Dales. Note that the roads and tracks shown are not necessarily rights of way. The roads covered in detail by each route are shown by heavier lines. Principal tracks which might draw the interest of the cyclist are shown as dashes where rideable and dots where not. This is subjective depending on factors such as the weather as much as the rider and ignores the effects of gradients. It is probably best to work on the rule that cycles can be taken over tracks shown with dashes without any real difficulty while those shown predominately with dots are best avoided. Although a number of the better tracks are described in detail these are not really suitable for tourists with a full load of luggage, but aimed more at the day tripper or mountain bike rider who is keen to get away from motor traffic and does not mind a bumpy ride, occasional push, or wet feet.

The maps in this book are perfectly adequate for road navigation, but in order to get the best appreciation of the topography the Ordnance Survey *Routemaster* sheet (1:250,000, or about 4 miles to the inch), together with the 1:50,000 sheets for those areas to be visited at length are recommended. These latter maps are especially useful as they show rights of way and are essential for any 'off the road' cycling. Sheet 98 — *Wensleydale and Wharfedale* — is indispensable in this respect. The best cycling maps ever produced were the Bartholomews *Half Inch* series and their successors on the 1:100,000 scale, with their contour shading giving the clearest indication of the hilliness of each road. The southern part of the area is still available as the *West Yorkshire Leisure Map*, but the old Sheet 35 covering the northern part of the Dales has not alas been reprinted. Older copies may still be found. On a local level the various inexpensive leaflets describing the more popular short walks are also handy and combine excellent maps with informative descriptions and background. These are available from information centres and elsewhere. Many villages display large scale maps and these can prove informative.

Rights of Way
Nearly every cyclist must, at one time or another, been tempted to take an inviting little lane, but has been deterred by the fear that it might be private. Although all public footpaths and bridleways are (or should be) signposted, there is no such requirement for roads. Thus there are many minor roads shown 'uncoloured' on the Ordnance Survey maps which are clearly not regular motor roads where the cyclist cannot tell if there is a right of way. Many old lanes, going back centuries, fall into this category, as do many upland paths, still technically roads which cannot be indicated as footpaths or bridleways. In practice, almost any byroad will be a right of way, except those which are obviously to serve a single farm or are private tracks to shooting moors. Signs which indicate a route unsuitable for motors are a sure indicator of a public road. The classification 'road used as a public path' has been legislated out of existence, such roads now being reclassified either as bridleways or as byways open to all traffic. While the highway authority is not obliged to bring this latter group up to a motorable standard, neither need any

bridleway be maintained to a standard suitable for cycling.

Motor cycles and other motor vehicles are not permitted on bridle-ways which are paths designated for the use of walkers and horseriders, both of which have a right of way. Since 1968 this right of way has been extended to pedal cyclists, who must however give priority to pedestrians and horseriders. This affirmation of rights long claimed by cyclists was only won after some opposition, and it is therefore appropriate to show due respect to other users, even if this means stopping to dismount. The fact that a path is a right of way does not give any user or group of users the right to cause a nuisance and to do so is an offence. Public attitudes to cycling are very susceptible to inconsiderate behaviour of cyclists, both in town and country. At a time when cycling groups are campaigning for improved facilities, inconsiderate behaviour by other cyclists is likely to hamper their efforts.

It is perhaps worth mentioning that it is not actually against the law to cycle on a footpath (except where a specific 'No Cycling' ban is in force, or along a footway adjacent to a carriageway) but the rider may be liable to a charge of 'reckless, careless or inconsiderate' cycling, as by its very nature pedestrians would be assumed to have uninterrupted use of the path. Furthermore, a cyclist may be turned back by a landlord or tenant, as no right of way would exist — not that this is ever likely to happen on the remoter upland paths. The hill farmer has a living to make and provided you do not hinder him (such as by leaving gates open, or damaging walls) he is unlikely to hinder you. It should be noted that although access land is generally closed to the public at certain times of the year, rights of way across such land are not affected.

Dales Roads

The earliest roads would have existed only in the traveller's memory: a recollection of an easy place to ford a river, the best side to skirt a mire or an outcrop of rock indicating the best place to cross into the next valley. Gradually a worn path would be created encouraging more traffic; a bridge would replace the ford, a causeway would be built across wet ground, a waymark stone would guide travellers across the moor. In such ways almost all our present-day tracks and roads were born. Wheeled transport was still unheard of. Carriage of goods would be by packhorse or packman, or that now forgotten but versatile form of transport, the sled.

The earliest trackways almost invariably kept to high ground, as the valley bottoms presented obstacles in the form of vegetation and bog. In many cases these older ways can still be followed, as along the shoulders of such valleys as Wensleydale and Swaledale. Roman interest in the Dales was limited, but their splendid road from Ribblesdale to Wensleydale survives and can easily be followed by bicycle.

It was during monastic times that the use of the road network grew with the establishment of commercial and agricultural interests by the monks in areas often remote from the parent houses. These interests included farms, cornmills, even mines, and regular lines of communication developed. The Dissolution of the Monasteries in the sixteenth century resulted in a reorientation of travel patterns and a loss of the driving force behind improvements to the road network.

Not until the second half of the eighteenth century, with the spread of turnpiking to the main roads, did carts and carriages become a practicality. Initially it was the old roads which were turnpiked, still following their direct hilly courses, but later roads were built anew — the first to be deliberately created on any scale since the Romans. The Enclosure Acts of the late eighteenth and early nineteenth century parcelled out dale and fell alike. It is hard to imagine the countryside without its network of stone walls marching up the hillsides oblivious of gradient. Many old tracks were diverted and enclosed while others were created as recalled in names like Intake Lane or Occupation Road.

The Dales today have escaped over-attention of the road engineer and have not had their character sacrificed to cope with the needs of motor traffic. Some have never been given a modern tarred or asphalt surface and constitute the famous 'green' roads which are such a prominent feature of upland Britain. No cycling trip to the Dales would be complete without venturing along at least one. Indeed a bicycle is about the only practicable way of exploring many of them, as they are so remote from motor roads. Several green roads have a prepared stone surface generally firm or smooth enough to cycle along and in this book a metalled road has been used to describe these, though nowadays this term is usually taken to mean a tarred road. An excellent historical background is provided in *Roads and Trackways of the Yorkshire Dales*, by G.N. Wright (MPC, 1985).

It must be said that riding these upland tracks can be a wearying experience. Excellent and perfectly firm sections can abruptly end in churned-up and muddy ditches that require time-consuming circumnavigation. Back-breaking ascents can be followed by bone-shaking descents that have one longing for smooth tarmac under one's wheels — they are not everybody's cup of tea. For those, however who are bitten by the bug and delight in getting 'far from the madding crowd' the area offers unlimited scope for exploration. All the principal green roads are, of course, described in this book, while many more are marked on the maps with an indication of their difficulty.

Although mountain bikes are ideal for this sort of terrain, any old bike is perfectly adequate — in fact the older the better! Mountain bikes gain through their ability to insulate the rider from the worst of the innumerable bumps and jolts experienced on hill tracks and some minor roads. If you are not riding the latest product of technology do not despair, all these routes were covered on a standard touring bike.

There are a few general problems associated with cycling in the Dales. One is the steepness of the descents which, as emphasised below, requires a really dependable machine. A second is the sometimes poor condition of the roads themselves. On many minor roads the surface can be broken up and loose in places, while road grit can accumulate along the edge of the carriageway, particularly on hills and bends. This is a special problem in winter and spring following wet weather. Under these conditions steering, let alone braking, can be impossible and so all descents should be made with great caution. Ice can also linger where shaded by stone walls, long after its presence has been suspected. Another hazard is sheep which have no more road sense than the average pedestrian and, when startled, can run in any direction. There are usually a few lurking behind walls at cattle grids ready to bolt out in front of unsuspecting cyclists. On enclosed roads try to avoid driving sheep along in front of you: given the opportunity they will beat a retreat.

Equipment

This is the point where most cycling books explain about all the essential bits and pieces without which any tour is doomed to failure. In fact, with the possible exception of gears, almost any bike will suffice, providing you are happy with it and everything is in tip-top condition. In particular your life will depend on brakes which can be trusted for strenuous use day after day.

A couple of weeks before setting off on any tour give the bike a thorough overhaul, replacing any brake or gear cables that show sign of fraying. Make sure you have brake blocks of modern materials which give better stopping power in the wet than the old plain rubber type. Tyres will wear more quickly under heavier than usual loads, especially on poorly-surfaced byways. The best protection against punctures are good tyres, properly inflated.

Gears which are suitable for everyday cycling in flatter parts of the country will almost certainly be too high for touring. Dales' hills are wars of attrition, and a rock-bottom gear of down to about 30in will prove its worth not only while ascending but in fewer aches and pains at the end of the day. If you do not know how to calculate gear ratios your local cycle shop will explain and fit you a lower set. If fitting a new freewheel yourself, make sure your derailleur can cope with any wider ratios.

All new components should be given time to bed in and prove themselves. While there are some excellent cycle dealers in and around the Dales many areas are remote so mechanical breakdowns can present more of a problem then elsewhere, especially as public transport is so sparse. Again prevention is better than cure.

Getting to the Dales

There are only two civilised ways to travel, and taking your bike on the train enables you to enjoy both. Many cyclists from far afield will use rail to get within striking distance of the Dales but here the first difficulty arises. The area lies between the East Coast and West Coast main lines and on the former there are tight rules on the conveyance of accompanied bicycles. It is ironic, but given present restrictions the easiest route to the Yorkshire Dales from the south of England is via Lancashire! Current rules are that whereas cycles can be taken on most East Coast Main Line trains, cycle accommodation must be pre-booked, though this can sometimes be done up to a few hours before travel. A bicycle ticket must also be bought. An increasing number of cross-country 'Express' services, operated by 'Sprinter' diesel units, now require pre-booking though weekend restrictions on both Inter-City and Express routes are less severe. Booking can be a considerable deterrent to using rail, as you may be unsure which day, let alone which train, you may wish to travel on. Against this the booking system does mean that you can be assured of cycle accommodation, at least as far as anything on British Rail can be certain. The number of cycles per train is also limited.

At the moment there are no restrictions or charges on West Coast Main Line services or through Liverpool-Leeds-Newcastle trains (but not 'Express Sprinter' services), or on the few non-Inter-City 125 trains from the Midlands to Leeds and York. The position with rail services is always likely to change, especially with the imminent completion of the East Coast Main Line electrification. British Rail produce a booklet, available from any major station, covering restrictions on the conveyance of bicycles on long-distance services, but this does not list many local services such as those in West Yorkshire. All those through Leeds are operated by the latest 'Pacer' or 'Sprinter' diesel units on which cycles, although allowed in principle, are not easily accommodated (particularly on Pacers), and are banned in rush-hours. It is best to check before travel by ringing Leeds (0532) 448133.

The East Coast Main Line provides railheads at York, Thirsk, Northallerton and Darlington. Apart from the A1 and possibly the A59 York-Knaresborough road, cyclists should not find traffic on the main approach roads prohibitive. York, of course, is a popular tourist centre in its own right and a tour of the Dales can be preceded or followed by a few days in that city. Some notes on the road approaches from York are given in Route 11. There is also a rail link from York to Knaresborough and Harrogate. From the south and Midlands, Inter-City services also run to Leeds. Although all main roads from that city are busy there are local rail services to Ilkley, Skipton and Harrogate.

The West Coast Main Line has railheads at Preston and Lancaster, though from Scotland the longer approaches from Carlisle or Penrith provide excellent cycling through the byways of the Eden Valley, including the Cumbria Cycleway. Both Preston and Lancaster have good cycling links to the Dales. In fact the North Lancashire Cycleway can be utilised from either. From Preston there is also a rail link to Colne which is within easy reach of Skipton or Malham. From Lancaster the branch line to Skipton provides a number of setting-off points for Ingleton, Settle etc.

From the Manchester area an interesting approach is by rail or road to Hebden Bridge, then over the moors to the Brontë village of Haworth. The steam-operated Keighley and Worth Valley Railway is the easiest way on to Keighley, beyond which one crosses into Wharfedale at Addingham. This hilly route will get you into shape for the Dales, especially if you try the direct road from Keighley to Ilkley, over Rombalds Moor (Route 1).

The only rail service to actually penetrate the Dales is the famous Settle and Carlisle line, which after a fiercely fought campaign has survived another closure crisis. The recent reopening of local stations and improvements in train frequency vastly increased its usefulness and in turn the large increase in custom helped to swing the decision against closure. Cyclists have benefited enormously from this improved service, arguably more than walkers, as it puts the whole of the Dales within their reach without the need to traverse the busy approach roads from West Yorkshire. Dentdale or Wensleydale — *terra incognita* to most day riders — are now brought within a few hours train ride of Leeds, while Swaledale and even Teesdale are within the scope of a day trip. This line too will in due course go over to 'Sprinter' operation and so expect to have to book.

As well as the scheduled train services from Leeds there are additional charter trains on certain weekends from Preston and Blackburn over the Settle and Carlisle line. For details write to Yorkshire

Dales National Park, Colvend, Hebden Road, Grassington, Skipton, North Yorks BD23 5LB. Please enclose SAE.

Youth Hostels

Youth Hostels provide friendly and informal accommodation for travellers with a limited budget. They are graded according to the facilities offered and vary from purpose-built hostels such as Hawes to converted schools and cottages. Dormitory accommodation is provided. Meals can be purchased at most hostels while self-catering facilities are always available. An address to contact for information can also be found in the back of this guide.

There are about fifteen hostels in and around the Yorkshire Dales National Park, most in the popular walking areas. These tend to be full for much of the summer and advanced booking is advisable. The eastern part of the Dales is less well served which makes it more difficult to be covered satisfactorily.

Yorkshire Dales Cycleway

This is a signposted route embracing all the major dales within the National Park, keeping almost entirely to minor roads. This does mean that it utilises some of the toughest inter-valley crossings so despite its modest length (about 135 miles) it represents quite a challenge. All parts of the way are, of course, covered in this book, together with places of interest on and adjacent to it.

The relevant sections are:

Skipton to Linton	Route 2
Linton to Malham and Settle	Route 3
Settle to Ingleton	Route 18
Ingleton to Dent	Route 19
Dent to Hawes	Route 23
Hawes to Wensley	Routes 22 and 26
Wensley to Grassington	Route 30
Grassington to Skipton	Route 2

It is hoped that the official adoption and promotion of the cycleway will lead to better facilities for cyclists. Further details can be obtained from the National Park Centre at Grassington or the CTC.

ROUTE 1
LOWER WHARFEDALE: OTLEY to ILKLEY, BOLTON ABBEY and GRASSINGTON

Distances from Otley (miles): **Burley** $2^1/_2$, **Ilkley** 6, **Addingham** 9, **Bolton Bridge** $11^1/_4$, **Bolton Abbey** $11^3/_4$, **Barden Tower** $14^3/_4$ (Appletreewick $17^1/_4$), **Burnsall** 18, **Linton** $20^1/_2$ (Threshfield $21^1/_2$), **Grassington** $21^1/_2$.
Distances from Appletreewick (miles): **Burnsall** $1^3/_4$, **Hebden** 3 (Grassington $4^3/_4$).

The road from Leeds to Otley (11 miles) is a good one. Follow cycle-route signs for the university, then A660 Skipton. Although rising continuously to the city boundary the gradients are steady and there is a splendid descent into Wharfedale. An alternative route from Leeds runs via Kirkstall Abbey and Guiseley, saving a mile to Burley, but this is a busier road and built-up nearly all the way.

Cyclists from Bradford can join this route at Burley (10 miles) or take the very hilly minor road from Shipley via Baildon. This road passes the 'Cow and Calf' rocks on its descent to Ilkley. Although a more scenic route, this road carries an enormous amount of motor traffic at weekends. For a note on the rail services from Leeds to Ilkley see page 13. From Keighley there is an excellent road via Silsden to Addingham (8 miles), or the direct moor road to Ilkley (see below).

INTRODUCTION

To many Yorkshire folk the Dales means Wharfedale. It is the valley most accessible from the densely-populated south of the county. It leads past idyllically-situated villages below graceful hills to the depths of an unknown mountain hinterland. The river is picturesque everywhere, sometimes a sedately flowing stream, elsewhere a convulsing torrent. No one can claim to have visited the Dales if they have not visited Wharfedale.

Although the longest of the Dales, Wharfedale is never monotonous. It changes in character as the river pursues its course, beginning as a moorland stream, then as a sparkling cascade over the limestone floor of Langstrothdale, a mature river down its straight glaciated valley to Grassington, then feeling its way through confining hills to Bolton Abbey where it emerges into a gentle and gracefully curving vale for the remainder of its course. It is near Otley that the river leaves what might be termed true 'dales' scenery and so therefore this town has been (rather arbitrarily) chosen as the starting point. This is not to deny that the lower reaches of the river, past Wetherby and Tadcaster, are through good cycling country.

This chapter covers the section of Wharfedale from Otley via Ilkley and Bolton Abbey to Grassington, the uppermost part of the valley being described in Route 4 following. As may be inferred, this is a road to be avoided at weekends on account of tourist traffic, but at other times it can be surprisingly quiet. There are byways on the north side of the river as far as Bolton Bridge which can be recommended to the rider, but those higher up are more popular with motoring tourists.

THE ROUTE

Otley is a pleasant town, with a busy market, half a bypass and a fine position amid Wharfedale. There are some riverside gardens at Otley with boating, etc. At nearby Farnley Hall the artist, Turner, was a frequent visitor. The town is sheltered by the long ridge of the Chevin, from which a fine view of Wharfedale is obtained, and it can be reached from the old Leeds road.

Between Otley and Ilkley the easier road is the busy A65 through Burley, but running along the north side of the valley is a very pleasant alternative, via Askwith, which provides much the better cycling. It leads directly into the minor road via Nesfield to Bolton Bridge, but the visitor should first cross the river into Ilkley.

Some distances from Otley (miles): **Leeds** 11, **Bradford** 10, **Keighley** 11 (14 via Shipley), **Pateley Bridge** 16 (Route 6), **Fountains Abbey** 19 (Route 6 or 7), **Harrogate** $11^1/_4$ (Route 7), **Harewood** $8^3/_4$, **Wetherby** $14^3/_4$.

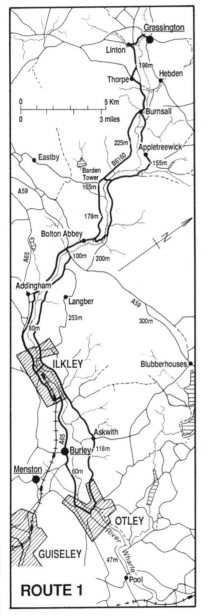

ROUTE 1

There is a lot more to **Ilkley** than first meets the eye. Although an important centre in Roman days the town did not develop until Victorian times, first as a spa and then as a residential dormitory for Leeds and Bradford, enabling the well off to exchange the smoke of the cities for the purer air of Wharfedale.

Keeping to the main A65 nothing of note is seen save the old manor house, just past the church. This has been restored and is now a museum. By turning up at the traffic lights the main shopping street, The Grove, is reached, which retains a hint of elegance from more leisurely days. Victorian Ilkley stretches up the hill onto Ilkley Moor, which is actually part of the much larger Rombalds Moor, stretching from Skipton to Menston.

The direct road from Ilkley to Keighley ($6^1/_2$ miles) crosses Rombalds Moor, attaining a height of 380m. About a mile is left untarred on the Ilkley side of the summit. Being a dead-end for motorists it is not signposted, but from Ilkley turn up Wells road, near the station, bearing left once above the town. From Keighley leave by Bradford Road, turning left opposite East Riddlesden Hall (National Trust). At the hilltop bear left into Banks Lane, then second right into Ilkley Road.

The river at Ilkley should not be neglected. There are some pleasure gardens near the old bridge, just upstream of the main one, and boating on the Wharfe. Just across the river is the minor road through Nesfield and Beamsley to **Bolton Bridge,** which is a delightful cycling route up the valley.

The main road from Ilkley runs to Addingham. On the way it is as well to turn off onto the parallel old road (signposted Sandbeds), which is traffic-free. After skirting Addingham the B6160 is a pleasant tree-lined road to Bolton Bridge.

North of Bolton Bridge there are again two roads — one major, one minor — running up the valley. However the minor road turning out of the A59 a little to the east and running via Storiths up Wharfedale cannot be recommended. It is extremely hilly and does not pass within view of the priory. Its upper section can most handily be gained by the footbridge at the Cavendish Pavilion (see below).

Bolton Abbey — strictly speaking a priory — dates from the twelfth century. The entrance is near the post office and there is no admission charge but donations for the upkeep of the church are welcome. Most of the building is in ruin but it still retains the shell of the great east window of the choir which adds so much to the dignity of the whole. The nave is still in use for worship as the parish church, while the remainder fell into gradual decay after the Dissolution of 1538. The west tower, started in 1520, was never completed.

The attractiveness of the priory lies not so much in the ruins themselves, but in their beautiful situation on a low grassy bank on a bend of the river. The Wharfe may be crossed by the footbridge and, by cutting up the steep bank opposite, the best views of the priory are obtained.

The section of Wharfedale from Bolton Abbey to Grassington (10 miles or so) is one of the most scenic in the country and classic tourist ground. As well as beauty it is rich in history and legend. By simply keeping to the roads good views of the valley are obtained, but the best scenery, including the famous Strid, lies along the banks of the river and can only be explored on foot. By turning out of the main road at the Cavendish Memorial, a little north of Bolton Abbey, a long driveway takes one down to the entrance to **Strid Woods** and the Cavendish Pavilion (refreshments), a popular rendezvous. A wooden bridge here provides a useful link to the minor road up the east side of the valley, particularly for those coming south who will need to cross here to visit Bolton Abbey.

Strid Woods, which extend from here nearly to Barden Bridge, form part of the Devonshire Estate and so are private property. Visitors are welcome, however, and waymarked footways which have been laid out can be enjoyed

Bolton Abbey

for a small contribution to their upkeep. The walk to the Strid and back will take about an hour by a well made path and is charming throughout.

At the Strid the river rushes through a cleft in the rock only $1^1/_2$ or 2m wide, but many times deeper. As a spectacle it can be disappointing in dry weather. The strength of the current can be gauged by comparing the width of the river here and just below. Do not attempt to jump across — lives have been lost. The walk can be extended to the aqueduct footbridge, about half a mile beyond the Strid or to Barden Bridge (about the same distance further), and a return made by the path on the far side of the river. However this path can get very wet below the Strid and is not suitable for those without stout footwear.

Another short walk, which will occupy from half an hour to half a day, is to the Valley of Desolation. The path turns out of the east side road $^1/_4$ mile north of the Cavendish Pavilion (a path cuts off the corner from the bridge). The walk is a popular one, forming the first stage of the ascent of Simon's Seat. Those with more modest ambitions will enjoy a pleasant stroll to the edge of Posforth Gill and make their way down to the waterfall they espy amid the trees. This rocky glen is the Valley of Desolation, so-called because of the havoc caused by a severe storm last century. A more idyllic spot to linger in could hardly be imagined now.

Returning to the main road at the Cavendish Memorial, the road

northwards gradually ascends, giving a good view of Barden Fell, the
dominant hill in this part of the valley. In a couple of miles is the upper
entrance to Strid Woods, which offers a shorter but less attractive
pedestrian route to the Strid itself. The main road then drops to a narrow
bridge before rising to meet the direct road from Skipton ($5^1/_2$ miles,
Route 2) a little short of **Barden Tower**.

Barden Tower falls in the category of romantic ruin. It originated as one of
a number of hunting lodges around the boundaries of the old forest of
Wharfedale. Part of the building is now a restaurant while the adjoining barn
offers 'bunkhouse' accommodation.

Barden Bridge, just below the tower, is an ancient structure, with pretty
views up and down the river. An inscription on its eastern approach notes
that it was 'repaired at the charge of the whole West Riding 1676'. Before
Grassington rose in importance Barden Bridge carried the main road from
Skipton to Pateley Bridge.

At Barden Tower a decision has to be made whether to continue
direct to Burnsall, along the B6160, or to take the minor road crossing
Barden Bridge which loops round through Appletreewick. The choice
is a hard one as both have considerable merit. The main road certainly
has the finer views as it rises some way above the valley floor, and the
prospect of Burnsall, clustered around its bridge and perfectly framed
by the surrounding hills, is one of the most well known in the Dales. The
alternative road is intrinsically the more appealing, but it takes a cyclist
(not a motorist) to appreciate its twists and turns. This is the road taken
by the Yorkshire Dales Cycleway. Beyond Barden Bridge it rises to
meet the road up the east side of Wharfedale and, continuing north,
offers delightful glimpses as it works its way round a side valley. At a
T-junction, where the road to Appletreewick turns left, the branch right
leads to Skyreholme, a quiet backwater of Wharfedale, and up to the
Pateley Bridge road.

The lane through Skyreholme drops to a fork, from which there is a distant
view of Parcevall Hall, high among the woods across the valley. Although
the site has long been occupied, the present building was rebuilt this century
in the form of an old manor house. It is now used as a diocesan centre. The
gardens, open to the public from Easter until October, contain many unusual
plants.

For Trollers Gill cycles must be left by the bridge below the entrance
to Parcevall Hall. From the bridge a path runs up the typical limestone
valley, over a disused dam, and bearing right at an old signpost. A little
further on it bears left, following the stream which runs underground higher

Cyclists at Cavendish Pavilion

up. Here Trollers Gill is entered, a narrow defile of overhanging limestone cliffs reputedly haunted by the Barguest, a giant spectral dog. The gill continues for about $^1/_4$ mile or so before widening out and losing its individuality. The return to Skyreholme must be made the same way.

As an alternative to the regular road from Appletreewick to the B6265 for Pateley Bridge, the lane through Skyreholme may be taken. This is tarred for about a mile, nearly to the junction of tracks north to Stump Cross and east over Pockstones Moor. Both of these tracks are, in the main, rideable but involve slow crossings over uninteresting moorland.

Appletreewick is one of the most prettily-situated of Dales' villages and nearly all its buildings exhibit some feature of antiquity or quaintness. It needs to be explored at a walker's pace rather than a cyclist's, otherwise much of interest will be missed. Taken as a whole the village has been overpraised: it lacks the photogenic core of some of its Wharfedale rivals. From Appletreewick it is a delightful run of a couple of miles to Burnsall, where the main valley road is rejoined.

Burnsall proves as attractive on close inspection as it does from afar, with old cottages huddled along its twisting main street and its village green bordering the river. At the far end of the village is the old grammar school, now a primary school, which dates from Tudor times.

Beyond Burnsall the roadside walls provide the evidence that a limestone district is being entered, which embraces the remainder of the Wharfe Valley except for the very gathering grounds of the river. The road works its way onward with somewhat trying gradients among smooth-topped hills and rising some way above the Wharfe. Two diversions from the direct road can be made: the first to **Thorpe**, an old-world hamlet tucked away amongst the folds of the hills and, a little further on, to **Linton**. This showpiece village is a must, its green dissected by a clear stream crossed in turn by stepping stones, a clapper-bridge, ford, footbridge and Victorian roadbridge. Picturesquely situated round the green are the Fountaine Inn, some old cottages, the impressively styled almshouses and the Youth Hostel. Do not miss the pretty cluster of buildings on the opposite side of the main road.

Coming up Wharfedale motor traffic for Grassington is signposted round via Threshfield, but there is a shorter way, by turning right at Linton crossroads (straight on from Linton village). This road drops to the Wharfe where a turning leads to Linton's ancient church. From Grassington bridge there is a steep hill up to the centre of the little town.

Grassington is a unique place. A side turning opens out into the attractive square and the narrow main street, winding up the hill. Along it is a jumble of old buildings in the warm local stone while there are quaint peeps into side lanes and ginnels. Its development really began with the expansion of lead mining on the moors above the town, but its central location, amid the finest scenery in Wharfedale, has ensured its survival as a tourist centre. There is a very interesting museum in the square and some good short walks about Grassington. A visit to the National Park Information Centre, on the Hebden road, will give some ideas.

About a mile north of the town, and reached by a turning (Garrs End Lane) out of the main street, are Grass Woods, an area of special scientific interest. There are a number of waymarked paths through the woods. A return may be made by dropping down to the Conistone road and returning along a riverside path which comes out at Grassington Bridge. On the Wharfe about a mile from the town is Ghaistrill's Strid, where the river tumbles over a rocky ledge in its bed.

Just below the town are Linton Falls and Linton Church. These can be reached by road, turning left immediately on crossing the bridge, or by a footpath out of the Hebden road, just past the information centre. The falls make a pretty sight and a little further is Linton Church, which mostly dates from the fourteenth century.

It is appropriate that the main street of Grassington lies not along any of the through roads, but instead heads up to the moors where much of

Barden Tower

the former wealth of the town came from. The lead mines were systematically expanded in the eighteenth and nineteenth centuries and the workings cover several square miles around Yarnbury. Little now remains on the surface, save for the conspicuous smelting chimney and the network of old flues and watercourses. The area is mainly of interest to industrial archaeologists, the climb from Grassington being likely to put off most cycling tourists. A leaflet describing a history trail is available from the information centre in Grassington and although aimed at those exploring on foot, cyclists should have little difficulty in reaching the places described. The tracks across the moor are mainly rideable but not all are rights of way.

Some distances from Grassington (miles): **Skipton** 9 (Route 2), **Gargrave** 8, **Malham** 11 (Route 3), **Kettlewell** $6^3/_4$ (Route 4), **Hawes** $22^1/_4$ (Route 5), **Aysgarth** $20^1/_2$ (Route 4), **Leyburn** $24^1/_4$ (Route 30), **Pateley Bridge** $10^1/_2$ (Route 12).

ROUTE 2

SKIPTON to WHARFEDALE

Distances from Skipton (miles):
Via Bolton Abbey: **Embsay** $1^3/_4$, **Bolton Abbey** 6, **Barden Tower** 9,
Appletreewick $11^1/_2$, **Burnsall** $13^1/_4$ (Cracoe $17^3/_4$), **Linton** $15^3/_4$,
Grassington $16^3/_4$.
Via Cracoe: **Rylstone** 5, **Cracoe** 6 (Threshfield $8^1/_2$, Kilnsey $11^1/_2$),
Linton 8, **Grassington** 9.

INTRODUCTION

Skipton rightly claims the title of 'Gateway to the Dales' and lies within easy reach of the queen of them — Wharfedale. The principal road linking them is the B6265 from Skipton to Grassington, which is the most direct way to the upper part of the valley around Kettlewell. This means, however, that perhaps the finest part of Wharfedale is missed, that between Bolton Abbey and Grassington. The Yorkshire Dales Cycleway wisely takes in Bolton Abbey on its way from Skipton and so this will be the route first described, followed by the direct Skipton-Grassington road. This latter road is often busy with quarry traffic.

Skipton has a strong 'country town' air about it, being the centre for a wide rural district, including much of Wharfedale. At the same time it has an affinity with industrial Yorkshire and Lancashire, and retains the Tuesday early-closing of a typical mill town. At the head of the broad main street is the parish church near which, but almost hidden away, is Skipton Castle. This is open to the public daily. Building began in the eleventh century and later it became a possession of the Cliffords, a notable local family. The castle was besieged and severely damaged in the Civil War, but later rebuilt by the redoubtable Lady Anne Clifford. The Leeds and Liverpool Canal runs through the town, with a branch terminating below the castle. Boating is a popular and colourful holiday activity.

The Town Hall houses the Craven Antiquities Museum of the area, Craven being the name given to the district north-west of Skipton embracing the watersheds of the Aire and Ribble.

Some distances from Skipton (miles): **Keighley** 9, **Bradford** 19, **Colne** 12, **Clitheroe** 19, **Settle** 15$^1/_2$ (Route 14), **Malham** 11 (Route 14), **Ilkley** 9$^1/_4$.

THE ROUTE

Via Bolton Abbey

The easiest (or rather the less difficult) way to Bolton Abbey from **Skipton** is via the main A59 and Bolton Bridge. The tourist route turns out of this road on the hill out of the town to **Embsay** where, at the bottom of the village, is the headquarters of the Embsay Steam Railway. This has reopened part of the old Skipton-Ilkley line and is busy working to restore services as far as Bolton Bridge. Embsay is now mainly a commuter village for Skipton, but one local industry is quarrying.

Taking the lower road from Embsay (the upper road, via Eastby to Wharfedale, is described below) the lunar landscape of the quarries is skirted by a good level road to the hilltop village of Halton East. The road onward, narrower and quieter, drops down a little side-valley to emerge at Bolton Abbey village. The entrance to the abbey, or rather priory, is almost opposite, at the 'hole in the wall'. For a description of the priory see Route 1.

The section of Wharfedale from Bolton Abbey to Grassington is described fully in Route 1, so the following information is intended to merely set out the options for the cyclist. Continuing north from Bolton Abbey brings one to the Cavendish Memorial where a driveway leads down to the entrance to Strid Woods. At the refreshment pavilion a footbridge leads across the Wharfe to the minor road up the eastern side of the valley. If visiting the Strid cycles can be left at the pavilion or at the upper entrance to the woods, a few miles along the main road. At the hilltop beyond this road meets the direct road from Skipton.

For Barden Tower and the main road to Pateley Bridge (10$^1/_2$ miles) see Route 1.

Cycling from Skipton to Barden Tower direct is 5$^3/_4$ miles. From Embsay the road rises to and through Eastby, with a stiff climb to its summit (311m) where there are good views. The descent, especially fine in autumn, leads over the moors to join the B6160 just before Barden Tower.

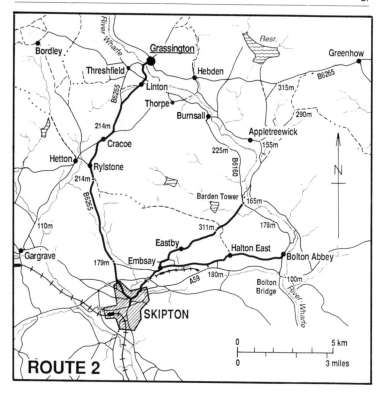

Above Barden Tower the choice is between two very attractive roads. The longer but unclassified one through Appletreewick probably has the edge, and is taken by the Yorkshire Dales Cycleway. Both roads lead to **Burnsall**, one of the most prettily-situated villages in England. Beyond Burnsall one can retrace one's route over the bridge, doubling back to reach Grassington via Hebden, or take the main road, now running through limestone country, to Linton. Just off route is the tiny hamlet of Thorpe, from which a little-used road leads to Cracoe.

This minor road is taken by the Yorkshire Dales Cycleway, heading for Malham. Though very narrow it is tarred throughout. It runs below distinctive conical hills, 'reef knolls', thought to have been formed when the area lay under a warm sea. For the continuation from Cracoe to Malham see Route 3. Burnsall to Skipton this way is $10\frac{1}{2}$ miles, to Malham $12\frac{1}{2}$ miles.

The Fountaine Inn at Linton

Linton, a prizewinning village, lies just off the Burnsall to Thresh-field road, which is crossed for the direct but unsignposted road to Grassington, a mile further.

Via Cracoe

There is nearly a mile ascent out of **Skipton** to the bypass. Thereafter the road is much easier for the while, with good views of the gritstone edge of Rylstone Fell. Conspicuous on the skyline is a cross, raised to commemorate the peace of 1813 and, at a lower level, are the ruins of Norton Tower. The Nortons were a powerful northern family in the sixteenth century and the tower was a summer retreat.

Afterwards the road rises, revealing an extensive view over the hill country towards Malhamdale as a descent brings one to the village of **Rylstone**. This village is dissected by the present road, so little more than the mill pond and the cluster of cottages around it will be noted. A mile further is **Cracoe**, where a pleasant side-road from Gargrave (5 miles) comes in. On Cracoe Fell stands another landmark, the local war memorial. For the road via Thorpe to Burnsall see above.

The main road dips to run past the cement works — entering, of course, limestone country — and to the fork of the Linton and Thresh-field roads. For Grassington the Linton road is preferable, as described in Route 1. For Wharfedale above Grassington see Route 4.

ROUTE 3
GRASSINGTON to MALHAM
and SETTLE (CIRCULAR)

Distances from Grassington (miles): **Linton** 1, **Cracoe** 3,
Hetton $4^1/_2$, **Airton** $8^1/_2$ (Settle direct $14^3/_4$), **Malham** 11, **Settle** (via
Kirkby Malham) $17^1/_2$.
Return distances from Settle (miles): **Malham Tarn** $6^1/_2$ (Arncliffe
11), **Street Gate** 8, **Kilnsey** 13 (Grassington $16^1/_2$), **Grassington**
(direct) $14^3/_4$.
Distances from Malham (miles): **Arncliffe** $8^3/_4$, **Kilnsey** $6^1/_2$.

INTRODUCTION

The scenery around the village of Malham is the most interesting and
spectacular in the Dales, and its name is well known throughout the
country. Malham Cove, a sheer limestone cliff 90m high, is of course
its most famous attraction, but there are several other notable features
in the locality. To take in all the sights one must abandon the cycle and
resort to shanks' pony, and allow the best part of a day.

Malham is not a cyclist's paradise. The only easy approach is up the
winding lane from Gargrave, in many ways a delightful ride, but the
amount of traffic it has to carry at weekends is unbelievable. Malham
Tarn is only a few miles from the village, but at a much higher level, so
a trip to it is not to be considered lightly unless proceeding beyond. All
in all this is an area where a careful study of the map beforehand will
save tears later.

Lying as Malham does between two important tourist centres,
Grassington and Settle, a circular route has been selected embracing the
three. The outward route is via Hetton passing south of the higher
ground, returning via Malham Tarn. There are some advantages in this
arrangement: those going no further west than Malham can pick up the

return route at Malham Tarn, while the hilly terrain lends itself more to the day rider than those impeded with full touring paraphernalia. Also of the links between Malham and Wharfedale only the road route via Arncliffe is really suitable for the heavily loaded. A decision on the final leg of the return trip can, of course, be taken on the spot to suit time and energy available. The accompanying map is at a larger scale than most to show the network of bridlepaths.

THE ROUTE

There are two ways from **Grassington** to Cracoe — via Threshfield or via Linton. For the latter which is more interesting, turn left immediately on crossing the Wharfe Bridge. Linton village (Route 1) is one of the prettiest in the Dales. The main Skipton road is joined near the cement works and followed for 2 miles to just beyond Cracoe where the Gargrave road is taken. This is a very pleasant byway but only followed to Hetton where another side turning leads over the hill to Winterburn, a secluded hamlet. Half a mile south is Friar's Head, a remarkably fine example of a seventeenth-century house with splendid stone mullion windows. From Winterburn the road rises and falls a few times to Airton, where the main tourist route to Malham is met.

From Airton, Settle is $6^1/_4$ miles by the direct road which rises a total of 220m. At its mid-point it joins the road from Kirkby Malham described below. Another way to Settle, for those who cannot face such hills, is by a charming lane through Otterburn to Hellifield ($3^1/_2$ miles), where it is 6 easy miles to Settle, mostly by the busy A65.

Both **Airton** and its neighbour **Kirkby Malham** can boast odd corners to catch the visitor's eye. Indeed either village is as cameraworthy as Malham itself, but scarcely noticed by the onward traveller. The hilltop beyond Kirkby Malham reveals Malham Cove and village which, as likely as not, is entered past a long line of vehicles overflowing from its car park.

Malham bears up well to its tide of visitors and manages to retain its charm. There is a venerable inn, various souvenir shops, a couple of cafés and a Youth Hostel. The first port of call should be the National Park Information Centre to obtain information on the area and to acquire a footpath map.

The two principal walks are:
To Malham Cove (approximately 2 miles there and back). This is reached by a broad path which turns out of the Arncliffe road a little north of the village. Rustic steps conduct the army of visitors up to the limestone

Kirkby Malham Church

pavement which extends across the lip of the cove. In returning, a diversion to the very foot of the cove should be included and a return to the village made by a path down the eastern side of the valley.

To Gordale Scar (2-2$^1/_2$ miles). There is a motor road as far as Gordale Bridge, but cycles are as well left in Malham, as on foot the return can be varied. From the far side of Gordale Bridge a path leads north to the mouth of the gorge, a collapsed cavern, up which it is possible to scramble (it is easier up than down!). The path beyond continues up to Malham Moor, so unless really energetic return to Gordale Bridge. On the opposite side of the road a path leads, in just a few paces, to Janet's Foss, a pretty waterfall, and by continuing alongside the stream the Pennine Way is met a little south of Malham and followed back to the village.

   NB The above two walks can be combined by taking the direct path from the top of Malham Cove to Gordale Bridge. Take care to keep to the right of way and do not damage walls.

   It will have been observed that the land to the north of Malham is much higher than that to the south. This relative uplift follows the line of a geological fault — the Mid-Craven Fault — which runs east-west just north of the village into which the valleys of Malham Beck and Gordale are cut. **Malham Tarn**, about 2$^1/_2$ miles to the north, is at an elevation of 375m above sea level, about 175m higher than Malham and reached by a choice of two hilly roads. The Yorkshire Dales Cycleway takes the eastern of these, skirts the tarn and then runs to Settle via Stainforth. For those following the cycleway (not returning to Grassington) this is fair enough, but the route via Catrigg Force (Route 17) to Stainforth is recommended. The vicinity of Malham Tarn and the various routes beyond to Littondale and Wharfedale are described below.

Malham to Settle
Return down the valley to Kirkby Malham, where there is a turning right. The Settle road climbs steeply, joining the road from Airton just before the final moorland summit (386m). On the descent beyond, the road dips to cross Scalebar Bridge, on the far side of which a path leads to Scalebar Force, just below the road. The bridge stands about 150m above the town of Settle, but most of the descent is concentrated in the last $^3/_4$ mile where the road plunges down at 1 in 5. Settle is entered by the older, higher part of the town. For a description of Settle see Route 14.

NB There is an excellent bridleway route from Malham to Settle, via Stockdale. This is described under Route 17.

Settle to Malham Tarn
From Settle the Horton road is followed for a mile or so to Langcliffe where, beyond the green, the road climbs steeply (up to 1 in 5) for half a mile. Near the top, where the road bears left, a track straight on leads to Victoria Cave, the most impressive of a number in these limestone hills.

The track is followed uphill for half a mile and then a footpath on the right taken. Five minutes' walk will bring one to the mouth of the cave. The above track, incidentally, continues as a bridleway to Malham, but it is a dull crossing and not one for misty weather. It is preferable to return to the road and resume the route below.

Beyond the turn the road continues to climb, but at a much easier rate. No dull moorland road is this, for it jinks through terraces of bare limestone, while there are excellent views over the deep valley of the Ribble. Both Ingleborough and Penyghent are prominent. Just before the road becomes enclosed again a track on the left comes up from Stainforth, via Catrigg Force (Route 17). Then, after dipping into a little side-valley, there is a long dreary pull to the junction with the motor route from Stainforth. There is still a bit of climbing to do before the watershed is crossed, whereupon Malham Tarn is seen ahead situated

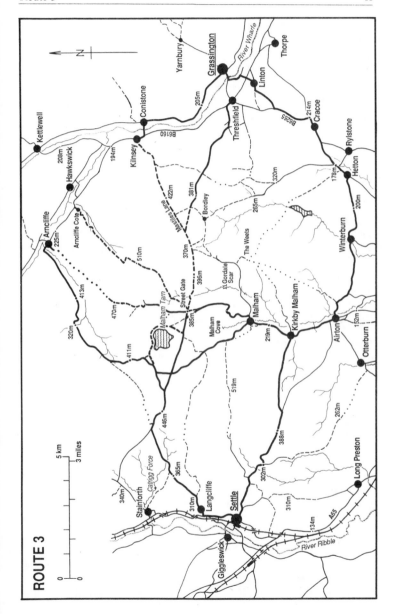

ROUTE 3

on its bleak upland plateau. If wishing to make a circuit of the lake watch out for a turning left in half a mile (the Arncliffe road). This joins the road up from Malham village and a little further on a driveway on the right leads to Tarn House.

> Malham Tarn owes its existence to a flat shelf of impervious rock that is exposed among the overlying limestone. The environs of the tarn are dreary, the only saving grace being the wooded limestone cliffs that provide a background to the lake and house. Tarn House is a Victorian mansion now used as a residential field study centre while the borders of the tarn are a nature reserve. The driveway past the house is a bridleway, but please show consideration for other users as it is a popular walk.

The driveway rejoins the direct road across the moor, passing south of the tarn, at Street Gate, though strictly speaking the bridleway bears right to join this road near the outfall from the tarn. Malham village can easily be reached in 10 minutes or so by either of the roads down from the tarn, but both are very steep in their later stages and the cyclist should watch out for pedestrians.

Street Gate is a sort of Clapham Junction of tracks in the middle of nowhere. It is the starting point of the various routes leading to Wharfedale or its tributary, Littondale. These will be described in turn, starting with the road route from the tarn to Arncliffe.

To Arncliffe by road
By road from **Street Gate** $7^1/_2$, **Malham** $8^3/_4$, **Settle** 11 miles.

From Water Houses, north of the tarn, there is a slight rise followed by a gradual ascent along the curving flank of Fountains Fell. The scenery is more impressive in scale than content with the surroundings rather bare save for some isolated farms and sheep pastures. All this descent must be paid for, as beyond Darnbrook the road rises sharply (1 in 5) to regain its lost height. There are glimpses into the precipitously-sided Cowside Gill before a steep and lengthy fall to Arncliffe. The views up and down Littondale, when it is safe to admire them, are magnificent. From Arncliffe to Grassington is $7^1/_2$ miles and to Kettlewell $5^1/_2$ miles. Both Littondale and Upper Wharfedale are covered in Route 4.

To Arncliffe via Middle House
Allow about 2 hours from Street Gate.

This is not classified as a bridleway throughout its length and there are a great many stiles to cross, so overall this cannot be recommended despite its scenic interest. It also has its history as it formed the Monk's

On the bridleway beside Malham Tarn

Road from Malham Tarn to Arncliffe.

Follow the access road to just before Middle House Farm, where a gate is passed through on the left, and bear right to meet a track zig-zagging up from the farm. On the skyline is a gate, beyond which keep slightly to the right to come alongside a wall dipping to Middle House. The way is then straightforward as far as a small tarn, passed on the left, to a wall and stile. To this point the track has been good and generally rideable, but hereon it is no more than a rough footpath between a succession of stiles — about ten in all — in the walls that march down the hillside and disappear into the depths of Cowside Gill. The path descends only gradually, over limestone terraces, with a very steep and awkward final drop to Arncliffe.

To Arncliffe via Arncliffe Cote
Allow about $1^1/_2$ hours from Street Gate.

The track, over springy turf throughout, offers no hazards for the cyclist. It is clear enough to be unmistakeable, yet has not suffered the fate of so many unmetalled tracks churned up by the use (and misuse) of motor vehicles. It is interesting in that for most of its course it is untrammelled by enclosure walls and so is perhaps more typical of an ancient 'green' road than many others.

From Street Gate it heads north-west to an awkward ford (after which keep right), then slants uphill keeping a remarkably direct course over rolling moor. At the very top bear right to and through a wicket gate. After another gate a brow is reached overlooking Cote Gill, a tributary of Littondale. Here it swings round to the left, dropping into the head of a small valley, where it turns sharp right to head down the valley bottom. It is then plain sailing for the remaining couple of miles down to Littondale. The deep gorge of the Cote Beck, just on the right, is worth a peep. The track finally bears left to cross a subsidiary stream then continues down the bare hillside before zig-zagging to the end of the lane coming up from the bridge on the Arncliffe-Kilnsey road. From here it is $1^1/_2$ miles to Arncliffe, 4 to Kettlewell and 6 to Grassington.

The only difficulty southbound is spotting the abrupt turns mentioned above: after passing an old lime kiln on the right keep straight on at the gateway in the wall beyond. The track turns left and uphill about 300m further.

To Kilnsey and Grassington via Mastiles Lane
Allow about 1 to $1^1/_2$ hours from Street Gate to Kilnsey.

Twenty-five years ago a proposal to properly surface this as a motor route was strenuously and successfully opposed and it remains an excellent example of 'green' road. It forms part of a very old upland way running east-west across the Yorkshire Dales, linking Fountains Abbey with its property in Cumbria. Until the 1760s, when the moors were enclosed, its line was waymarked by several crosses, of which only the bases now survive.

From Street Gate the track, rather optimistically signposted Grassington, heads east alongside a wall. After fording Gordale Beck (footbridge) it continues across the closely-cropped turf to a gate where it becomes enclosed. In another half mile the direct route from Malham village comes in.

The road up from Malham crosses Gordale Bridge then rises precipitously for the best part of a mile before levelling out. Where the road ends at a farm keep straight on, following a rough cart track to meet Mastiles Lane in $^3/_4$ mile. This section of the way rejoices in the name of Smearbottoms Lane. Westbound the turning to Malham is not signposted. It turns out of Mastiles Lane in a dip shortly after a gate and is accompanied by a wire fence. This road from Malham passes near Weets Top, on which is a restored waymarking cross. Bog trotters may like to try the tracks from it down to Airton or Hanlith.

Mastiles Lane

The next section of Mastiles Lane is much better surfaced, with the old metalling in reasonable condition. Various tracks lead south to the unseen farmstead of Bordley at the head of the Winterburn Valley. At the end of the enclosed section an important junction is reached, for here the branch track to Grassington bears right, keeping company with the wall.

This branch track, after 10 minutes over bumpy turf, becomes a tarred road leading down to Skirethorns, near Threshfield. It is the quickest way off the moor in bad weather, but take care on the steeper sections. One can also cut over the hill to Bordley, from where a cart track heads south. This soon improves and later becomes a tarred road to Hetton.

Mastiles Lane itself, keeping to the wall on the left, is unsurfaced and rather cut up, but in half a mile becomes enclosed again at Mastiles Gate. What is undoubtedly the best part of the road follows, winding over the bleak upland with a good firm surface. On reaching its summit (422m) a distant view of Wharfedale is obtained and a long descent follows, loose in places but all rideable with reasonable care. The village seen ahead is Conistone. Eventually Kilnsey is reached, from where it is about 4 miles to Grassington, 3 to Kettlewell.

ROUTE 4
UPPER WHARFEDALE: GRASSINGTON to KETTLEWELL and AYSGARTH

Distances from Grassington (miles): **Conistone** 3, **Kilnsey** $3^1/_2$ (Arncliffe $7^1/_2$, Halton Gill 12), **Kettlewell** $6^3/_4$, **Starbotton** $8^3/_4$, **Buckden** $10^1/_4$, **Cray** $11^3/_4$, **West Burton** 19 (Leyburn $26^3/_4$), **Aysgarth Falls** $20^3/_4$, **Aysgarth village** $20^1/_2$.

INTRODUCTION

This route covers the whole of Wharfedale and its tributaries above Grassington, together with Bishopdale which forms its main link with Wensleydale and Walden. While there is a more direct road from Upper Wharfedale to Hawes, over Fleet Moss, the more roundabout way via Aysgarth is worth the extra distance. Similarly this is a more interesting and varied route to Leyburn than the slightly shorter road through Coverdale described in Route 30.

Approaching Grassington from the south it will be noted how the valley contracts just above the town. Here the river flows through a gorge in similar fashion to and at the Strid, near Bolton Abbey. Continuing north, however, Wharfedale assumes a remarkably uniform and straight profile, extending to Buckden and beyond, providing ten of the easiest and best cycling miles in the Dales. This same profile is exhibited by the tributary valley of Littondale, which joins just above Kilnsey, and makes it a profitable detour on the way up Wharfedale. Assuming then that the cyclist will be visiting Littondale the route described will be via the Conistone road to Kilnsey, Littondale, and then the continuation up Wharfedale to Kettlewell.

The scenic attractions of this route are excellent and while there are no points of special interest each village passed through exhibits some quaint nook or other, and a cluster of old cottages which will attract the

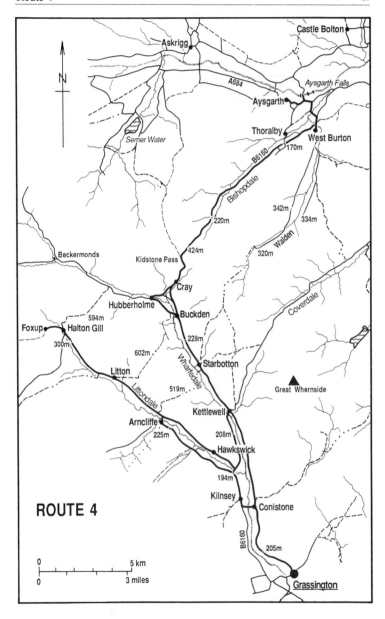

eye and camera. There are several old inns en route to slake any thirst, not that there is much chance of working one up before the Kidstones Pass.

THE ROUTE

From **Grassington** it is preferable to take the Conistone road, which in a mile or so skirts Grass Wood and drops to the Wharfe, a good view opening up ahead. A footpath doubling back leads to some very pretty riverside scenery above Ghaistrill's Strid (Route 1). **Kilnsey Crag** is conspicuous ahead from the road on to Conistone. This is only a tiny place, but its church is reckoned as one of the oldest in the Dales. For Kilnsey and Littondale the valley has to be crossed here, but those heading direct to Kettlewell will find the minor (unsignposted) road a delight. For the path over the moors from Nidderdale to Conistone see Route 10.

The little village of **Kilnsey** nestles under the hillside south of its famous crag. Here was a grange of Fountains Abbey, well placed where Mastiles Lane (Route 3) reached Wharfedale. Part of the old manor hall survives as a farm building. Kilnsey Show is one of the principal outdoor events in Wharfedale. Kilnsey Crag, which towers 50m over the road, was formed by the undercutting action of the ice of the Wharfedale glacier. A little further on is the junction of Wharfedale and Littondale, a tributary watered by the little River Skirfare.

The side valley of **Littondale** provides a pleasant digression and is worth an hour or so of anybody's time. It rises only gradually in the 7 or 8 miles to Halton Gill. Littondale may thus easily be visited on the journey up Wharfedale: as a bonus as far as Arncliffe ($3^1/_2$ miles) there are parallel roads permitting a variation on the return. The central part of Littondale, around Arncliffe and Litton, is perhaps the most charming. **Arncliffe** is the largest settlement in the Dale and consists of a number of old buildings around an extensive green. The church, which makes a fine picture from the bridge, has been much restored but inside there is a record of the local men who fought at the Battle of Flodden in 1513.

From Arncliffe a bridleway runs north to Starbotton, good on the Littondale side, but poor on the descent to Wharfedale. The views are fine but hard earned.

The Arncliffe to Malham road begins with 2 miles of ascent, partly at 1 in 6, followed by a tricky descent to Darnbrook. All this downhill has to be retrieved as the road climbs up the flank of Fountains Fell before it drops once more to Water Houses, where the bridleway skirting Malham Tarn may

Kilnsey

be taken before dropping down to Malham village. As a route from Arncliffe to Settle this is more interesting (and shorter) than that via Halton Gill (Route 15) but involves more ups and downs. For a fuller description see Route 3.

Continuing up the valley there is a gentle rise to **Litton**. Why this village should have given its name to the dale, the old name of which was Amerdale, is not clear. Here are the last shop and inn in the valley. There is a well defined bridleway over to Buckden (about $1^1/_2$ hours), along which cycles can easily be taken. Just beyond the village a long and conspicuous track climbs the hillside to join the road from Halton Gill to Settle, but the longer route is easier. By Halton Gill the valley has opened out and is noticeably barer. This hamlet, 300m up, was an important staging point on the old packhorse road up from Settle which continued over Horse Head Moor to Langstrothdale, described in Route 15. This incidentally, is the easiest of the three bridleway crossings from Littondale to Wharfedale or Langstrothdale.

Halton Gill is a tiny place but most of its few buildings can tell a story. Its former school is dated 1626 and attached to what was the chapel. The valley road continues a little further to Foxup, but by now the charm of Littondale has given way to dour gritstone moors and fells. It is possible to take the bridleway over the watershed to Horton in

Arncliffe church

Ribblesdale (Route 17), but it is a long, lonely and very wet crossing.
It would be far better to turn around and, with the prevailing gradient in
your favour, return down the valley to Wharfedale. From Arncliffe the
northern side of the valley may be adhered to, taking the lane through
the pretty hamlet of Hawkswick. Arncliffe to Kettlewell is $5^1/_2$ miles.

On rejoining the B6160 north of Kilnsey the road climbs a little way,
then keeps high along the valley side for the 2 miles to Kettlewell. The
result is an excellent view of the village on the descent to the bridge. In
1985 the bridge partly collapsed from frost damage, but has been
restored without impairing its appearance.

Kettlewell is the largest community in the valley north of Grassington, most of it lying back from the main road and so missed by the casual
visitor. Tourists are amply catered for with shops, inns, cafes and a
Youth Hostel. A stroll round the village will reveal no surprises, but the
quiet situation flanking its little beck will be envied. There are field
paths up and down the Wharfe from alongside the bridge.

The journey from Kettlewell to Leyburn, via Coverdale as a through route,
is scenically inferior to that via Buckden and Bishopdale to Wensleydale
(about 3 miles longer to Leyburn) and overall a fair bit hillier, including a
300m rise out of Kettlewell. Comparisons apart, however, it will be found
a rewarding road. The reverse way is described in full in Route 30. From
Wharfedale, rather than push up Park Rash, try the bridleway running east

from Starbotton to the summit of the Coverdale road. There are excellent views throughout.

Distances from Kettlewell (miles): **Carlton** $10^1/_2$, **Middleham** $15^1/_4$, **Masham** 24, **Leyburn** $17^1/_2$.

Beyond Kettlewell Wharfedale continues as before, steep-sided but with a broad level floor and marvellous scenery. The road is an excellent one rising only imperceptibly — perhaps the best cycling section in the whole of Wharfedale. Who said the Dales were too hilly! **Starbotton** is a pretty village, but the ruin on the skyline of an old lead smelting mill reminds us that in former days each of these now idyllic communities had to meet all its needs as best it could, and what now houses the holiday-maker once housed the miner.

A mile north of Starbotton look out for an old stone cross to the right of the road. It stands on the border of the onetime Langstrothdale Chase established in Norman times. At **Buckden** lived the verderers of the forest which had its own laws and punishments. Just above the village the valley forks. The minor branch is followed by the main road to Wensleydale, while stretching westward is Langstrothdale, as this uppermost part of the valley of the Wharfe is known. This bend and widening of the valley greatly add to the beauty of Buckden's situation and make it a popular walking centre.

Langstrothdale is very beautiful and the ride up it made so by the road and river running close together, for some miles immediately alongside. Even if continuing north via Bishopdale all should explore this valley as much as time permits — at least as far as Hubberholme Church which is very interesting — but preferably on to Beckermonds (5 miles from Buckden). The road is fully described in Route 5. The river descends over limestone steps and is a delightful companion. Above Beckermonds the valley loses its appeal, but one may continue either into Ribblesdale or over Fleet Moss to Hawes. If returning down Langstrothdale a short cut may be taken from Hubberholme Bridge to Cray.

Beyond Buckden the B6160 begins to climb out of Wharfedale with beautiful views. Cyclists plodding up the hill will not need to be told of the waterfall below the bridge at Cray: cyclists descending will most likely not spot it. Above Cray comes the steepest part of the ascent (1 in 6) as the road winds among the peculiar limestone terraces which are such a conspicuous feature of the landscape. Despite their battlement-like appearance they are purely natural in formation. Above them is the broad shelf forming the indistinct watershed between Wharfedale and

Bishopdale, known rather grandly as the Kidstones Pass. Prominent ahead is the Stake Road leading over Stake Moss to Semer Water and Bainbridge, as described in Route 5.

On descending into **Bishopdale** the warning signs, advising cyclists to take care, are well heeded. There are a lot of worse hills in the Yorkshire Dales but this has a record of accidents to cyclists: there are some straight sections linked by rather deceptive bends which may catch the unwary. The gradients are up to 1 in 6 again, as the road drops 220m in about $1^1/_2$ miles. A bridge marks the foot of the descent and a little further the Bishopdale Beck itself is crossed. The valley floor is now level, indeed the road is more or less flat for the next few miles before rising to a hilltop opposite Newbiggin. This hill explains the flatness of the valley as it once penned back the waters of a lake, the silted-up floor of which gives the valley its fertile strath. Another lake existed between Thoralby and the Ure, similar in formation to Semer Water.

Just beyond the Street Head Inn a decision on the remainder of the route needs to be made. For Aysgarth village, and Upper Wensleydale, the shortest route is via **Thoralby**. This is a trim little village with cycle hire available at the post office. After Thoralby there is a long ascent (1 in 6) up to Aysgarth. This involves some abortive climbing if heading for Aysgarth Falls or the Youth Hostel and in any case the more interesting way is to keep to the B6160 as far as West Burton. This is one of the prettiest villages in the Dales, but one must turn a little way out of the main road for it.

This side road follows the Walden Beck on which, at the entrance to West Burton, is a lovely dell backed by a fine waterfall. It is a pretty little spot, often quiet when nearby Aysgarth is over-run. A little further on is the village green, in the middle of which stands a massive obelisk putting all the other Wensleydale crosses to shame.

West Burton lies at the foot of Walden, but this deep valley does not lend itself to easy exploration by bicycle. The two roads up it are dead ends, terminating $4^1/_2$ and 3 miles respectively from West Burton, and both involving much uphill work on the way. Scenically the valley is similar to neighbouring Coverdale. Tracks, easily enough to follow in clear weather, cross the ridge to Bradley and Carlton, each about $1^1/_2$ hours from West Burton.

The Walden Head to Starbotton route ($4^1/_2$ miles, 2 to $2^1/_2$ hours) now starts on the far side of Walden Beck. It is rather a tedious climb, a grassy trod with a few marker posts. Above 560m this waymarked route crosses peat hags impassable by man or beast so veer slightly north to keep to easier

Kettlewell

ground. A good path runs due south along the 650m contour to the Boundary Gate, where it is an excellent descent, partly rideable, into Wharfedale. From the Boundary Gate there are also only three stiles between you and Kettlewell, though as far as Top Mere Top the ridge is very boggy.

Returning to the B6160 one will immediately admire the graceful bridge over the Walden Beck. The sign 'Unfit for Motors' will have many cyclists reaching for their maps, for across the bridge runs a fine green road which can be taken to West Witton or Middleham (Route 22). A little further on the roads to Leyburn and Aysgarth separate: by the latter Leyburn can be reached via Aysgarth Falls and Castle Bolton. This increases the distance by about 3 miles, but it is more of a tourist route than the direct road. From the junction with the A684 there is a stiff hill westward, near the top of which is the Aysgarth Youth Hostel and the turning leading down to the falls. These and all the other sights in Wensleydale are fully described in Route 22.

ROUTE 5
BUCKDEN to HAWES

Distances from Buckden (miles):
Via Fleet Moss: **Hubberholme** $1^1/_4$, **Raisgill** $2^1/_2$, **Beckermonds** 5,
Oughtershaw $5^3/_4$, **Fleet Moss** (summit) 8, **Hawes** 12.
Via Stake Moss: **Cray** $1^1/_2$, **Stalling Busk** (road junction) 7,
Countersett (Semer Water) $8^1/_2$ (Bainbridge $10^1/_2$), **Burtersett** 11,
Hawes $12^1/_2$.

INTRODUCTION

These two tough routes are rewarding links from Wharfedale to
Wensleydale. The Fleet Moss route, despite rising to the highest road
summit in Yorkshire, is the better for the general tourist, the old road to
Semer Water providing a bumpy ride over Stake Moss.

Buckden is the highest village in Wharfedale, about 10 miles north
of Grassington (Route 4). Although there are several settlements in
Langstrothdale which in olden times were self-contained communities,
the population of the valley is now very small. The place names found
— Hubberholme, Yockenthwaite, Oughtershaw etc — are Norse in
origin and record the early settlers. The whole area above Buckden
formed the medieval Forest of Langstroth, a wild area preserved for the
chase. Although the total rise from Buckden to Fleet Moss is about
360m, the initial stages of the journey are so pleasant that the general
upward trend will hardly be noticed. The real spadework comes beyond
Oughtershaw. Coming south there is a similar climb from Hawes, all
concentrated in the first 4 miles.

The alternative route described via Stake Moss utilises the direct
road to Bainbridge, one never improved for motor traffic, so still largely
as it was 100 years ago. Apart from the steep section up from the B6160
it will be found rideable, though requiring care on the long — very long
— descent to the end of the tarred road above Stalling Busk. As a short

cut to Bainbridge or Hawes it offers no appreciable savings over the longer route via Aysgarth; its advantage is that it passes Semer Water, which otherwise requires a hilly side-diversion from Wensleydale.

THE ROUTE

Via Langstrothdale and Fleet Moss

Turning out of the B6160 in **Buckden**, the narrow road runs across the level strath formed by the junction of two valleys. This is one of the most attractive parts of Wharfedale. Approaching Hubberholme the hills close in as Langstrothdale is entered. **Hubberholme** Church, across the river, forms a fine picture, but it is the interior which is of great interest.

To close the heavy door behind one is to shut out the passing of the centuries. The oldest parts of the church, including the tower, are transitional, the remainder dates from the fifteenth and sixteenth centuries. The rood-loft of 1558 is an extremely rare survival, one of only two in Yorkshire. Its destruction was ordered from York in 1571, but York was a long way away in those days and the reformers' zeal did not extend to these remote dales. The pillars and arches are unusual and in the pews there is an example of modern woodwork by Richard Thompson, the 'Mouse Man' of Kilburn. Opposite the church is the George Inn, the last house of refreshment before Hawes.

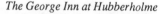

The George Inn at Hubberholme

Beyond Hubberholme the road winds up the narrow valley to **Raisgill**, the terminus of the track over from Halton Gill (Route 15). This formed part of a packhorse route which continued via Hubberholme Bridge and the Kidstones Pass into Wensleydale. A little beyond Raisgill the road descends to the riverside below the farmstead of Yockenthwaite. The next few miles past Deepdale alongside the infant Wharfe are delightful, the stream descending by a series of limestone steps and pools. The narrow verge between the unfenced road and river provides a linear picnicking area and also, unfortunately, a linear car park at times.

At **Beckermonds** the Oughtershaw and Greenfield Becks meet to mark the start of the Wharfe. Both these streams rise in the high gritstone country, with Beckermonds at the transition from 'valley' scenery.

The Beckermonds to Horton in Ribblesdale route via Green Field is 8 miles long and described fully in the reverse way in Route 17. The road is tarred as far as High Green Field, where it then continues as a metalled forestry road (bridleway) through the plantations, with Ingleborough appearing ahead. At the far end of the forest the road bears right: it cuts down to the end of the public road at High Birkwith but is not itself a right of way. The bridleway continues straight on, through a gate, soon being joined by the Pennine Way. It is then a bumpy ride down to Horton. At 395m this is the lowest crossing out of Wharfedale above Grassington.

From Beckermonds the Hawes road climbs steeply for a little way, then levels out as it passes through the hamlet of **Oughtershaw**. This has a nineteenth-century hall and an ornately-styled school of the same period.

It is beyond Oughtershaw that the slogging part of the ascent begins. The road rises a total of 240m in just under 2 miles, slanting up the bare fellside. Near the top a track left, below an old lime kiln, provides a short cut to the Roman road westward along Cam Fell. Finally, just after a steep left hand bend, the summit plateau is reached. Crossing it the extensive views south give way to those northbound, over to Wensleydale, with a brief glimpse of Semer Water. The road descends slightly to meet the Roman road which, a little further, carries straight on where the Hawes road plunges over the lip of the plateau into Sleddale — the final straw for cyclists coming south.

Fleet Moss to Bainbridge and Semer Water via the Roman road is a continuation of the road out of Ribblesdale, described in Route 17. It is all just about rideable down to Bainbridge and generally in good shape, but the long

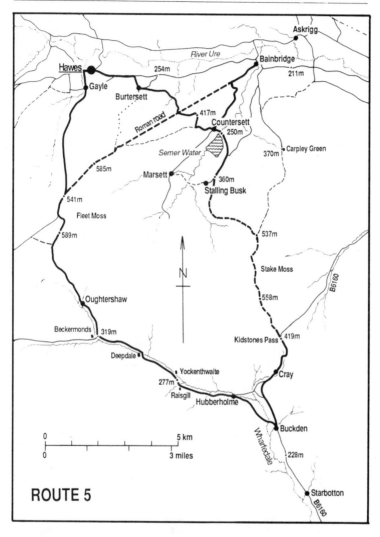

ROUTE 5

jolting descent is a poor way of avenging the climb to Fleet Moss. It is more or less level for the first 1½ miles to where, at a gate, it becomes enclosed again. From this gate a faint path runs north to Burtersett, but is not recommended. A little further on down the Roman road is an interesting bridleway which runs to Countersett. This turns off through a metal gate (no signpost) and swings round to head roughly east across the grassy tableland, eventually dropping to the road bend above Semer Water. There are some excellent views, but in poor weather any variations from the Roman road should be disregarded. This leads straight as an arrow down the bare hillside, with Askrigg seen dimly in the distance. The Hawes-Semer Water road, crossed halfway down, is the easiest route to either of those places.

The direct Hawes road from Fleet Moss, after the initial pitch at 1 in 4, drops more steadily — an exhilarating run — for a few miles, with a 1 in 6 descent into the hill village of **Gayle**, just above Hawes. Coming south, apart from the two steep sections mentioned, the road is merely an unbroken slog with little scenic relief. Overall the road rises 330m, one of the longest hills in the Dales.

Via Stake Moss and Semer Water
Allow about 2 hours between Buckden and Bainbridge. There is a long but scenically fine climb from **Buckden** via Cray to the top of the Kidstones Pass, a plateau of limestone falling away in a series of rampart-like crags above Wharfedale. There is no mistaking the Stake Road, keeping straight on where the B6160 bears right for the beckoning green pastures of Bishopdale. The road is rideable to the foot of a further series of limestone crags and very rough as it climbs through. On reaching the plateau above it becomes rideable again, in places running over the naked rock. The moor is remarkably flat and extensive, cutting out any northward views until after a few miles a secluded valley, **Cragdale**, opens up on the left. Hereabouts a track branches off to the right: this also leads to Bainbridge but is not recommended. The main track begins to descend and is still just about rideable, even though a bit touch and go in places. Further on it improves with good views over **Raydale**, the broad valley containing Semer Water (Route 22).

The start of the tarred road is met at the fork above the hamlet of Stalling Busk, beneath a timeworn finger post pointing back to Buckden. A little lower down the direct road to Bainbridge turns off to the right, contouring around the east of the valley before descending to that village. For Hawes keep straight on past the end of the lake, taking care on the rather dubious road surface.

Beyond the lake-end the road rises (1 in 4) to the little hamlet of Countersett where another road leads to Bainbridge. It then carries on uphill, a total rise of 160m above the lake. The reward is an excellent view of Upper Wensleydale and a downhill run the remainder of the way through Burtersett to Hawes.

ROUTE 6
OTLEY to PATELEY BRIDGE

Distances from Otley (miles):
Via B6451: **Farnley** 2, **Bland Hill** $5^3/_4$ (Fewston 7, Blubberhouses 9), **Dangerous Corner** $7^3/_4$, **Dacre** 11, **Summer Bridge** $12^1/_4$ (Brimham Rocks 14) **Pateley Bridge** 16.
Via Blubberhouses: **Blubberhouses** $7^1/_4$, **Thruscross** (inn) $9^1/_2$ (Greenhow 14), **Pateley Bridge** $14^3/_4$.
Add a mile if coming from Ilkley, via Askwith.

INTRODUCTION

Otley is a popular cycling rendezvous, being a main gateway from the industrial towns and cities to the unspoilt Dales. For a description of the town see Route 1. As well as being on the main route up Wharfedale it is the focus for a number of rather hilly roads that lead north to the Washburn Valley and Nidderdale. While this area provides great scope for those just out for a day's spin, anyone weighed down with a week's touring gear will make heavy weather of the hills and perhaps not appreciate its attractions fully.

The roads described below are the two routes from Otley to Pateley Bridge: never more than a few miles apart there is little to choose between them, though the slightly longer B6451 can boast more valley as opposed to moorland scenery. Both offer peeps of the reservoirs and woods of the Washburn Valley, but this cannot be explored thoroughly other than on foot. From Summer Bridge two very popular tourist attractions may be reached — Brimham Rocks and Fountains Abbey. The routes and distances to both of these are also included for completeness, as they are well within the scope of a day trip from Leeds or Bradford. It is perhaps worth mentioning that the lanes dropping down to Birstwith in Nidderdale offer a good alternative route to Brimham

Rocks, the climb out of the valley via Hartwith being much easier than the back-breaking hill north of Summer Bridge.

THE ROUTE

Via B6451
Just across **Otley Bridge** is the parting of the ways between the direct Pateley Bridge road and the B6451 which turns right and rises for some distance, skirting the grounds of Farnley Hall. Turning off through Farnley hamlet a continuous uphill follows before the road drops to the Washburn and the pretty Lindley Wood Reservoir. On the descent the cyclist will be sizing up the road ahead, climbing 160m to alongside the radio mast on Lindley Moor. The climb is steep, up to 1 in 6 at times.

On the ascent an inviting lane turns left (signposted Dob Park); this works its way round the hill to regain the main road beyond the summit. Although not saving any climbing — in fact the opposite — it offers excellent views over the Washburn Valley. At Scow Hall a bridleway cuts down to Swinsty Reservoir, a delightful little digression.

From the road summit there are good rearward views, in contrast to the dull tableland ahead, which is only relieved by a glimpse of Swinsty Reservoir on the left. Those with time and energy to spare may like to turn off to Fewston (Route 8), continuing to Pateley Bridge via Blubberhouses. As suggested above, those heading for Brimham Rocks may like to cut across via Kettlesing Head to Birstwith (about 12 miles from Otley), there picking up Route 9. From Birstwith on to Fountains Abbey is a hilly 8 miles (for the map see Route 13). As a through route from Otley to Fountains Abbey there is little to choose between this way and via Beckwithshaw and Ripley (Route 7): both go very much against the grain of the land.

After crossing the Skipton-Harrogate road at Dangerous Corner (an appropriate name given the speed of traffic, but one in fact dating back to coaching days), the B6451 skirts the Menwith Hill radio station to emerge high above the Nidd Valley, which provides some welcome scenic relief and the prospect of some downhill cycling. Nothing is ever straightforward in this part of the world, however, and after a steep drop to cross the Darley Beck there is a long toil before entering Nidderdale proper at Dacre Banks.

As well as serving Brimham Rocks the road north from Summer Bridge provides a useful route from Otley to Masham and Fountains Abbey etc. The road starts at 1 in 5, only easing when the top of the moor is reached. A mile or so further, beyond the crossroads, a track on the left leads up to the rocks, which occupy the highest part of the moor, nearly 300m up. For a description see Route 9.

Returning to the road this continues northward and is more or less level until the B6265 Pateley Bridge-Ripon road is reached. For Fountains Abbey this need only be followed for a mile before turning off for Sawley. The road on to the abbey is nearly all downhill. If heading for Masham, follow the B6265 to the Blackamoor Inn (2 miles) where a hilly road leads north via Grantley to Kirkby Malzeard, there joining Route 13. The alternative road from Summer Bridge to Kirkby Malzeard, via Wilsill, is comparatively dull and the same distance.

Distances from Summer Bridge (miles): **Brimham Rocks** $1^3/_4$, **Kirkby Malzeard** 10, **Masham** $14^3/_4$, **Ripon** (direct) $10^3/_4$, **Fountains Abbey** (via Sawley) 8.

At Summer Bridge the main road from Harrogate is joined for the last 4 miles or so to Pateley Bridge. Despite following the valley this again is somewhat hilly in its final stages. For Pateley Bridge see Route 9.

Via Blubberhouses

From **Otley Bridge** the road rises steadily for 2 miles before levelling out on the moor. There is a wide view in

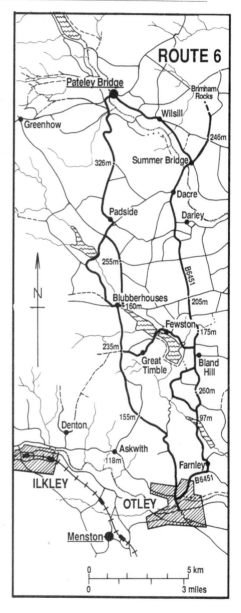

all directions, extending from the densely-populated belt to the south to the rolling hills ahead. After a few miles along a whale-back ridge a side turning runs across to Timble and Fewston (Route 8), situated in pretty reservoir-side scenery. Keeping to the direct road there are a couple of ups and downs before the final precipitous descent to **Blubberhouses** on the main Skipton-Harrogate road. The hamlet is nicely placed, and one wishes that there was more to detain the traveller before tackling the hills out of the valley. The name Blubberhouses is thought to be from blaw (blue) berry, but there are rival derivations.

Opposite the road from Otley a lane winds past Blubberhouses Hall and in half a mile turns north (ahead is the old Skipton road). This part of the Washburn Valley is especially beautiful, a deep hollow lined with trees and rocky crags, though spoilt by the extreme ugliness of the dam. The reservoir was completed in 1966 but for previous decades properties in the communities of the valley, Thruscross and West End, had been bought up and vacated and the fields allowed to return to waste.

The road further up the valley, apart from one or two pretty spots where it dips to cross streams, is moorland in character. One may continue either by the old road over Pockstones Moor to Wharfedale, or up to the Greenhow road — both are dull journeys. For Pateley Bridge cross the reservoir dam and continue up the steep hill to Thruscross.

At the east end of Blubberhouses the Pateley Bridge road turns up another long hill to regain the moor and the wayside inn at Thruscross. Here a misleading signpost indicates the way ahead, to Greenhow, as the recommended way to Pateley Bridge. You can save a good 2 miles by turning right, then next left through Padside. Despite being a more intricate route it is less hilly overall, though the gradients are steeper. After dipping into a side valley there is a mile of uphill which brings one overlooking Nidderdale at Guise Cliff, with the town of **Pateley Bridge** at one's feet.

On the right will be noticed a ruin, Yorke's Folly, reached by a short walk from the road. This may be continued along the top of the rocky escarpment as far as the TV mast, there cutting down for a return through the wooded undercliff. Hidden among the rocks and trees is the little Guise Pool. The road is regained beside a farm lower down the hill.

The descent from Guise Cliff is very steep (1 in 5), at the bottom joining a pretty lane from Glasshouses through Bewerley to Pateley Bridge. For Pateley Bridge see Route 9 and Upper Nidderdale, Route 10.

ROUTE 7
OTLEY to HARROGATE

Distances from Otley (miles):
Via Farnley and B6161: **Farnley** 2, **Beckwithshaw** $7^1/_2$ (Hamps-
thwaite $11^1/_2$, Ripley $12^1/_2$), **Harrogate** $10^1/_2$.
Via Pool and A658: **Pool Bridge** 3 (Beckwithshaw $9^1/_4$), **Weeton
Station** $5^1/_2$, **Buttersyke Bar** $8^1/_4$ (Knaresborough $14^1/_2$),
Harrogate $11^1/_4$.

INTRODUCTION

For this route there is a choice of two roads, one striking across the
eastern flanks of the Dales, and the other skirting them. The latter is, of
course, much the easier but is a busy road, particularly on the approach
to Harrogate. The road via Beckwithshaw, the old Dudley Hill
(Bradford) and Killinghall turnpike, is of more use to cyclists travelling
on to Ripley than to Harrogate.

Between these two roads are some interesting byways which might
be recommended to those in no particular hurry. Around Leathley, a
pretty village which can be reached from Otley by roads either side of
the river, is some fine park-like countryside with a network of narrow
lanes. One of these leads up to Stainburn's little Norman church and on
through Braythorn to the Beckwithshaw road. This is an ancient way,
worn deep between the fields. From Stainburn another road runs across
to Almscliff Crag, a rocky promontory affording spectacular views
over Lower Wharfedale. The main Harrogate road can then be gained
via North Rigton.

THE ROUTE

Via Farnley and B6161

After crossing **Otley Bridge** turn right and continue up a long hill to the

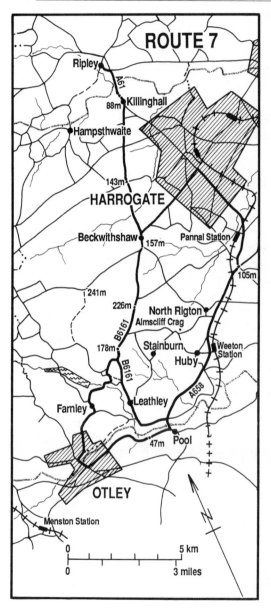

ROUTE 7

Ripley

A61

88m Killinghall

Hampsthwaite

143m

HARROGATE

Beckwithshaw 157m   Pannal Station

105m

241m

226m   North Rigton
B6161 Almscliff Crag

178m   Stainburn   Weeton
B6161   Station
       Huby

               A658

Farnley   Leathley

               47m Pool

OTLEY

Menston Station

0   5 km

0   3 miles

road junction at
Farnley. Here turn left
and take the next right,
the road dropping into
the deep and wooded
Washburn Valley. On
the left is Lindley
Wood Reservoir, a
popular area for walks.
After the precipitous
drop to the bridge there
is another steep climb
out of the valley as one
works up the network
of little lanes until the
B6161 (coming round
via Pool) is reached.
Heading south the di-
rect road to Otley is
signposted Lindley,
and easily missed.

The upper stages of
the B6161 are uninter-
esting and the views
featureless, apart from
a distant sight of Har-
rogate. A sweeping
descent leads to **Beck-
withshaw**. Here a
branch road — mo-
notonously straight —
turns off for Harrogate,
the last few miles being
all downhill. For Har-
rogate see Route 11.

Continuing north-
ward on the Ripley
road there is a steep
drop to Pot Bridge,
with care required on
the hill and the narrow
bridge itself. After a

corresponding rise to cross one last tongue of the moor a gentle descent brings one to Killinghall and the main A61 out of Harrogate. Ripley is a mile further, across the River Nidd. For Ripley and the roads up Nidderdale see Route 9, for Fountains Abbey Route 13 and for Ripon Route 11.

Via Pool and A658

This is an easy riverside run to **Pool**, an attractive village with large paper mills. It is 9 miles from Leeds and 10 miles from Bradford.

Beyond Pool Bridge the A658 is followed, a well engineered road with no steep gradients although a gradual uphill trend. This road to Huby was built anew about 1840 and its steady line can be compared with the old Pool to Harrogate turnpike (B6161) which merely improved old packhorse routes. The conspicuous rock outcrop to the north is Almscliff Crag. The busy A61 from Leeds is joined at Buttersyke Bar, 3 miles south of Harrogate. On the way note the graceful railway viaduct spanning the Crimple Valley which cyclists have to climb out of by a steep hill. The entry to Harrogate is by a gently descending slope. For the town see Route 11.

From **Spacey Houses**, a little north of Buttersyke Bar, a road runs via Follifoot to **Knaresborough**, and offers the cyclist a route to that town avoiding Harrogate. It passes near Plompton Rocks (Route 11). The new Harrogate-Knaresborough southern bypass, planned to open by 1992, will take a lot of undesirable traffic off these lanes.

ROUTE 8
HARROGATE to BOLTON ABBEY and SKIPTON

Distances from Harrogate (miles): **Kettlesing Head** 6, **Blubber-houses** 9, **Bolton Bridge** 15³/₄, **Bolton Abbey** 16¹/₄, **Embsay** 21, **Skipton** 22³/₄.

The recommended route from Harrogate, via Penny Pot Lane and Fewston, adds a mile to Blubberhouses and beyond.

INTRODUCTION

This route is a rather uninteresting road and also a fairly busy cross-Pennine link. Its main use for the cyclist is to connect Harrogate with Wharfedale, the finest parts of which lie north of Bolton Bridge. However this western exit from Harrogate provides a disappointing introduction to the Yorkshire Dales, as only on the dip into the Washburn Valley and the similar descent into Wharfedale is the scenery other than dreary. The upward trend and straightness of the roads also make them unappealing to cyclists, who are likely to be heading into the prevailing wind.

The high ground west of Harrogate formed part of the ancient Forest of Knaresborough, an area of uncultivated scrub and woodland. When the forest was enclosed and partitioned, following an Act of 1770, the opportunity was taken to lay out new roads, or straighten old ones, the consequences of which are recognisable on the map to this day. One of these roads became the Skipton and Harrogate turnpike road, now the A59.

As the A59 is the busiest road actually crossing the Yorkshire Dales it is best avoided where possible, which can be done easily enough as far as Blubberhouses by taking Penny Pot Lane. This runs parallel just to the south, and gives a peep of the pretty valley scenery around

Fewston. Another road from Harrogate might be mentioned, that via Beckwithshaw and Little Alms Cliff to Fewston, but this again is a generally uninteresting moorland road. If coming from the north via Ripley, rather than use the B6161 search out the bridleway to Hampsthwaite (Route 9) then work up the maze of lanes to join (or cross) the A59 at Kettlesing Head.

Beyond Blubberhouses the A59 must be used to Bolton Bridge. Here the tourist will turn off to reach Skipton via Bolton Abbey and Embsay.

THE ROUTE

Via Penny Pot Lane

This is the preferable road, being quieter, but no less uninteresting. Leave **Harrogate** by the north side of the Valley Gardens, which are signposted out of the main Ripon road (left at the traffic lights). At the gardens entrance bear right into Cornwall Road. After $^3/_4$ mile of uphill bear right again, still on Cornwall Road. This drops to cross the deep valley of the Oak Beck with a corresponding hill on the opposite side to bring one out onto the gently rising moor. The B6161 is crossed, then it is a case of switching on automatic pilot for the next 4 miles while the road runs almost straight across an uninteresting plateau. This is Penny Pot Lane,

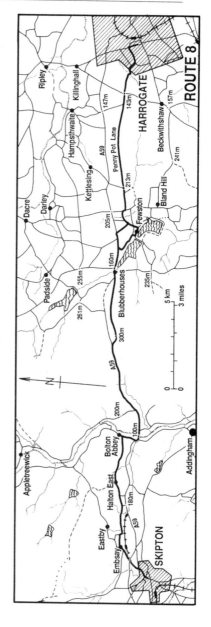

named after an old time inn, and a good if rather tedious example of an enclosure road.

On meeting the B6451 at a T-junction turn right then immediately left onto an unsignposted lane. Take the second right for the A59 and Blubberhouses. For Fewston and its pretty surroundings keep straight on instead.

Fewston, 8 miles from Harrogate, now consists of no more than an old church and a few cottages overlooking Swinsty Reservoir. This sleepy corner was once a busy village with mills in the valley, but the construction of the reservoir and the need to avoid pollution stifled its development. The round of the reservoir may be made by a good track, but this is a public footpath only. The road from Fewston to Blubberhouses runs through dense woods before turning up (1 in 6) to meet the main road. For continuation see below.

Via A59

Leaving **Harrogate** by the A61 a steep hill is crossed before one turns left onto the A59. This road rises almost continually for 3 or 4 miles to Kettlesing Head. A little further on the road picks up the line of a Roman road, providing a further 2-mile straight until the very welcome descent to **Blubberhouses**. This is amidst the very pretty scenery of the Washburn Valley, but there is nothing to detain the passing cyclist in the hamlet. Beyond Blubberhouses another long hill has to be faced, the road climbing up the steep-sided **Kex Gill** to emerge on the unenclosed moorland 300m up. The mining activity to the north, in these most incongruous of surroundings, is for silica sand.

The descent to Wharfedale is gradual at first, but then a modern section of road sweeps down splendidly to **Bolton Bridge**. The turning to Storiths, reached from the looping old road through Hazelwood, provides a short cut to Upper Wharfedale. This however, misses out Bolton Abbey. Near the foot of the hill, on the right of the main road, is the old Beamsley Hospital, some seventeenth-century almshouses. On crossing Bolton Bridge there is a first glimpse of the abbey.

From Bolton Bridge the main road leads direct to Skipton, hilly but still easier than the touring route described below. This turns up the valley to Bolton Abbey (see Route 1) then up a narrow and unsignposted road which is nearly all uphill to **Halton East**. Beyond that village there is the opportunity of cutting down to the adjacent A59, or continuing past the quarries to **Embsay**. This is the home of the Embsay Steam Railway (see Route 2). Beyond Embsay there is a rise to cross under the bypass, then a downhill run into **Skipton**. For the town see Route 2.

ROUTE 9
LOWER NIDDERDALE: HARROGATE to PATELEY BRIDGE

Distances from Harrogate (miles):
Via south side of river: **Hampsthwaite** 4^1/$_4$, **Birstwith** 6, **Darley** 9,
Dacre 10^1/$_4$, **Summer Bridge** 11^1/$_2$, **Wilsill** 13^1/$_2$,
Pateley Bridge 15^1/$_4$.
Birstwith to Summer Bridge (direct) 3^3/$_4$, **Brimham Rocks** 5.
Via Ripley and Brimham Rocks: **Ripley** 3^3/$_4$, **Burnt Yates** 6^1/$_2$
(Summer Bridge 10^1/$_2$, Pateley Bridge 14^1/$_4$), **Brimham Rocks** 11.
Brimham Rocks to Pateley Bridge 5.

INTRODUCTION

The amount of space in this book devoted to Nidderdale may appear generous, for what is after all only one of the lesser valleys in the Dales. However the area is rich in byroads and tracks and it is these that interest the cyclist; also the valley is within easy reach of several large towns and so deserves detailed coverage. In addition many guidebooks confine themselves to the National Park only, and so omit Nidderdale.

Nidderdale can be taken to cover all the river from Knaresborough to its source; this route covers the section from the outskirts of Harrogate to Pateley Bridge. It is quite an elusive river: roads cross but rarely accompany it and the terrain can be hard going for the rider. Against this there is plenty of good scenery and several places of interest to be found en route.

The usual approach from Harrogate is via Ripley and the B6165, which is also the route to Brimham Rocks, one of the strangest geological curiosities in Britain. A more pleasant way can be found up the south side of the valley, through Hampsthwaite and Darley, which is only slightly longer. By crossing the Nidd to the B6165 beyond

Birstwith the best of both worlds can be obtained, whether heading for Brimham Rocks or Pateley Bridge. Those coming from Knaresborough must travel via Ripley ($4^1/_2$ miles), a straight and rather dull road, though for Brimham Rocks there is an alternative way round via Burton Leonard.

THE ROUTE

Via south side of river

There is more than one road from **Harrogate** to the first village, Hampsthwaite, but probably the best is by leaving Harrogate by the Skipton road, turning right in $1^1/_2$ miles. This enters Hampsthwaite by Hollins Lane, a long downhill. From the opposite direction this is signposted Killinghall.

Hampsthwaite is one of a number of pretty villages in the Lower Nidd Valley, an area of fine rolling countryside with none of the monotony of the surrounding moorland. The village is popular as a dormitory for Harrogate, as are its neighbours. The Roman road from Ilkley to Boroughbridge crossed the Nidd near here.

Hampsthwaite is at the focus of a number of byways useful to the cyclist. From it radiate lanes to Beckwithshaw (4 miles), Kettlesing and Blubberhouses ($6^3/_4$ miles), Thruscross (7 miles), Bishop Thornton and Fountains Abbey (8 miles). There is also the bridleway via Clint to Ripley ($2^1/_2$ miles, see below).

West of Hampsthwaite the route continues with a steady rise for a mile or so, whereupon a turning leads down to **Birstwith**, another village in beautiful surroundings and with a graceful church. There are more pretty views as the road proceeds up the valley. About half a mile beyond Birstwith a track to the right (signposted Nidderdale Way) leads down to the river and the New Bridge, a fine structure dating from 1822. Return to the road which also drops to the riverside and a metal bridge. This is crossed by a private toll road (public bridleway) which provides a useful link to the B6165 and a short cut to Summer Bridge or (via Hartwith) Brimham Rocks. The road keeping to the south side of the valley runs alongside the river, then gradually rises to the village of **Darley**, which extends for a mile to the junction with the B6451. Without the cyclist being aware of it the road has parted company from the Nidd, and to regain the main valley there is a long hill to be surmounted to the hilltop hamlet of Dacre before a longer descent to the river at Summer Bridge.

Beyond Summer Bridge the road runs through pleasant wooded surroundings and then climbs to Wilsill. The last few miles on to Pateley

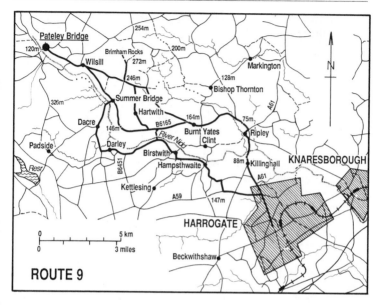

ROUTE 9

Bridge are quite hilly, the road threatening to head up the moorside in
one or two places before descending to the town. For Pateley Bridge see
below.

Via Ripley and Brimham Rocks

The road from **Harrogate** to Ripley, the busy A61, is a series of ups and
downs to Killinghall. **Ripley** is an individual sort of place, having been
totally rebuilt early last century in a heavy imitation French style,
complete with its own *hôtel de ville*. In the cobbled square are an old
cross and the stocks, other examples of which survive at nearby Clint
and Darley.

Ripley Castle, adjoining the village but screened by a high wall, has been the
seat of the Ingilby family for over 660 years though the building dates
mainly from the late eighteenth century. The south tower is older and has
been the scene of many historical events. The grounds and the castle are
open to the public on certain days in summer.

   The lane from the bottom of the village square is a bridleway and
provides a useful link to Clint and Hampsthwaite (2$^1/_2$ miles) across the
river. Part of it is on the line of a Roman road.

Beyond Ripley the road, the B6165, is level for a mile or so but then begins a long climb to the hilltop hamlet of **Burnt Yates**. This strange name is thought to be a corruption of Boundary Gates for it lay at the limit of land owned by Fountains Abbey. A little further on an important road junction is reached. Straight on is the old Pateley Bridge road, a little shorter than the present one and quite a reasonable alternative. Its main purpose now is as a route to Brimham Rocks, as will be described. The new road was built in 1826-8 to avoid the steep hills on the old, though in total travel time by bicycle there is hardly any difference between the two.

The main road — still known as New Line — continues with a long descent to Hartwith Mill (where a bridleway leads to and across the river) then rises to run along a hillside terrace, offering good views across the Nidd Valley, to Summer Bridge. It is then a hilly 4 miles to Pateley Bridge, through Wilsill.

The old road is easy at first, but following a dip into a little side valley rises for some distance culminating in a straight section over Hartwith Moor. From the crossroads with the route from Summer Bridge the road is easy to the turning for **Brimham Rocks**, which lie some way up a side track.

The location of the rocks, some way off the main routes and high above Nidderdale, may deter some cyclists from visiting them. Those who make the effort will not be disappointed. They consist of a vast number of grotesquely-weathered sandstone pillars, worn into comic outlines that scarcely seem to be the work of nature. Many have acquired nicknames from their appearance — the Turtle Rock, Dancing Bear, Druids' Altar etc.

When they first became known to the outside world their origin was put down to the Druids who got the credit for anything inexplicable to the historians of the eighteenth century. The modern explanation is that they are the result of erosion in an earlier and hotter climate of dry sand-bearing winds. The rocks now form a playground for youthful mountaineers and are intersected by a maze of paths which provide hours of exploration. Refreshments are available and the adjacent lodge is run as a National Trust information display and shop. From the escarpment behind the lodge there is a good view up Nidderdale.

The view eastward stretches across the Vale of York to the Hambleton Hills, on which the Kilburn White Horse may be discerned. The conical hilltop of Roseberry Topping may be picked out near the haze of Teesside. To the south-east the tower of York Minster is theoretically visible. Further south are the massive vapour clouds of the coalfield power stations — Yorkshire's own Spithead Review.

Some distances from Brimham Rocks (miles): **Otley** 14 (Route 6), **Masham** 13³/₄ (Routes 6 and 13), **Fountains Abbey** 7, **Ripon** 9³/₄ (Route 12), **Burton Leonard** 10¹/₂ (Boroughbridge 16, Knaresborough 16).

Brimham Rocks are about 5 miles from Pateley Bridge, the shortest way being south to pick up the old road from Ripley. There is a steep and long drop to Smelthouses — the name being a reminder that an old leadmining area is being entered — before joining the B6165 at Wilsill. There is one more hill before Pateley Bridge. The other route from the rocks, north to the Ripon road, is about a mile longer to Pateley Bridge but a reasonable alternative. Like the first road it is mostly, but not exclusively, downhill.

Pateley Bridge is situated on the slopes above the narrow valley floor. It is a natural centre for communications and a popular stopping point with visitors. It was formerly an important centre of the leadmining industry, and there is a small museum. The main tourist attractions in the vicinity are Brimham Rocks, described above, and the view from Yorke's Folly, on the direct Blubberhouses road almost opposite. Both are best visited en route to elsewhere, as they are tough cycle rides from Pateley Bridge. Slightly more accessible is the view from the old church at the top of the town. An easy and pleasant cycle route in the vicinity is along the Nidd Valley north of Pateley Bridge, as described in Route 10.

Some distances from Pateley Bridge (miles): **Masham** 13¹/₄ (Route 13), **Ripon** 11¹/₄, **Fountains Abbey** 8¹/₂ (Route 12), **Grassington** 10¹/₂ (Route 12), **Otley** 16 (Route 6).

ROUTE 10
UPPER NIDDERDALE: PATELEY BRIDGE to LOFTHOUSE

Distances from Pateley Bridge (miles): **Ramsgill** $4^3/_4$, **Lofthouse** $6^3/_4$ (Middlesmoor $7^3/_4$) **Scar House Reservoir** 11, **Horsehouse** (Coverdale) $15^1/_2$. **Lofthouse to Healey** $7^1/_2$, **Masham** $10^1/_2$.

INTRODUCTION

It is an odd fact that the only easy cycling in Nidderdale is to be found in its uppermost section, that above Pateley Bridge. The road then to Lofthouse is a delight, while the evenly-graded water authority road will take one with relative ease up to the bleak reservoirs at the head of the valley. The only regular road exit above Pateley Bridge is that from Lofthouse to Masham, but there are other ways open to the cyclist. The old cart road to Coverdale is quite practicable: there are other such routes across Fountains Earth Moor to Kirkby Malzeard, and the really determined might like to try the wild, and in part trackless route over to Conistone in Wharfedale. The valley itself includes a number of tracks but there are some frustrating anomalies apparent in the rights of way network.

When the boundaries of the Yorkshire Dales National Park were drawn up Nidderdale was excluded, partly because of the limited areas of public access. There are now moves to extend the park to include the valley which should do wonders for house prices. Scenically Nidderdale can hold its own with anywhere, and the vicinity of Lofthouse has long been known as 'Little Switzerland'.

The description below covers the road up to the head of the valley, commenting on the various side routes on the way. Then comes the road route to Masham, followed by some options for the cyclist who is prepared to foresake the modern roads.

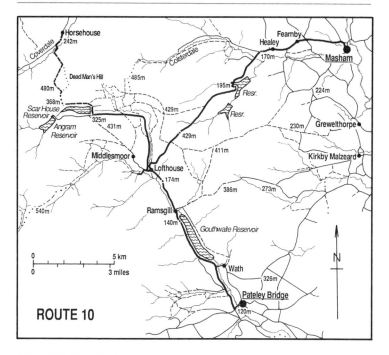

ROUTE 10

THE ROUTE

For **Pateley Bridge** see Route 9. For the first few miles up the valley there is a choice between the usual road, which keeps to the floor of the valley, and a hilly back way through Wath which is somewhat harder. On the bottom road is the Foster Beck Mill, which retains its enormous waterwheel. The mill processed hemp for the Knaresborough linen trade and is now a pub. The wheel remained in operation until 1967.

There is a pleasant road up the north side of the Foster Beck, becoming a track (bridleway) higher up. Here the valley has a wild beauty. The right of way fords the stream (a little tricky) below the site of the old Providence Leadmine and armed with a good map one can return to Pateley Bridge via the Brandstone Beck Valley or work up to the main road at Greenhow Hill. Gradients apart, all these tracks are rideable.

A little further on the side road from Wath joins, after which a slight rise leads to the foot of Gouthwaite Reservoir, the lowest of three built by the city of Bradford earlier this century. As it occupies the site of an old glacial lake it appears perfectly natural. Its immediate surroundings, between the road and waterside are a nature reserve (no access) and the reservoir is famous for the variety of birdlife it attracts.

An alternative to the road is a track (bridleway) on the opposite side of the valley between Wath and Ramsgill. From Wath a side road (no signpost) climbs steeply (extreme care is required on descent), then branches left; this soon descends as a cart track to run near the reservoir. At Covell Houses it becomes a road for the remainder of the way to Ramsgill.

The road alongside the reservoir is charming and, of course, level. A little way beyond is the pretty village of **Ramsgill**, with its venerable inn and small green. Ramsgill was a grange of Byland Abbey, far across the Vale of York, and an ancient agreement gave them rights to cross the lands of Fountains Abbey to reach this and other estates. From Ramsgill this road runs across the valley to Bouthwaite and over Fountains Earth Moor to Kirkby Malzeard (8 miles, see map). Nearly all is rideable but offers no scenic advantages over road routes such as Lofthouse to Masham.

Continuing up the valley a pleasant run brings one to **Lofthouse**. At the hillfoot before the village notice the River Nidd emerging from the rock, having run underground from Manchester Hole 2 miles upstream. A little beyond the village is one of the tourist highspots of Nidderdale, **How Stean Gorge**. This is reached by a side turn out of the Middlesmoor road. At a cottage tickets are obtained and the entrance to the gorge is nearby. It consists of a narrow canyon in the limestone, in places 20m deep, carved by the power of the How Stean Beck, a substantial stream. Paths, in places under the overhang of the rock, lead up the gorge and there are one or two caves which can be explored.

Middlesmoor rarely features on a cyclist's itinerary, being 120m higher than Lofthouse and, since the construction of the water authority road, effectively on a dead end. The view back down the valley from Middlesmoor is justly famous. For the routes from the village across to Wharfedale and over to Scar House and then Coverdale see below.

Lofthouse to Masham

This is the only motor road out of Upper Nidderdale. The gradients are more severe on the Nidderdale side (up to 1 in 4) but even so it is perhaps better to take this road eastbound to get the worst over with, as there are long uphills heading west. The ascent starts right in the middle of Lofthouse involving a mile of very steep climbing followed by a mile of plain steep climbing to the summit, 260m above Lofthouse. The reward is an extensive, but typically undistinguished, eastern view.

The road makes a gradual descent over the moor, passing an intriguing old guidestone pointing back to Kettlewell of all places! On the hills to the south are some sighting towers, built in connection with the reservoir conduits. There is a pleasant run along the waterside before an unwelcome rise to Healey. Before that village a side road branches off into **Colsterdale**.

This side valley of Colsterdale can easily be overlooked, but it contains a wealth of variety for its size. A road leads up it for about 3 miles to Colsterdale Head. A return may be made along the Coal Road, a good track along the south of the valley, to Gollingarth Foot.

West of Colsterdale Head a good track perseveres along the south side of the stream, closely paralleling the old bridleway. This track expires at GR 094797, on the north side of Steel House Gill. An hour's floundering over peat and heather would take you via South Haw to the Nidd Valley High Level Route (see below), still some way short of civilisation.

The only bridleway out of Colsterdale which can be recommended is north via Slipstone Crags and Witton Moor. This is a well defined path (not all rideable), presenting no problems. You may continue north to East Witton or down an excellent track to Ellingstring.

Just before Healey a road leads over the hill to Ellingstring ($2^1/_2$ miles) and the Masham-Leyburn road near Jervaulx Abbey ($4^1/_4$ miles). The road on from Healey through Fearby to Masham is nearly all downhill and an easy ride. For Masham see Route 13.

Lofthouse to Scar House Reservoir and Horsehouse (Coverdale)

The construction of the Bradford reservoirs led to a reorientation of the network of roads and lanes in that part of Nidderdale beyond Lofthouse. To some extent the road system is still in a process of change as patterns of farming and land-use alter. The main route up the valley formerly ran via Middlesmoor, over In Moor and crossed the Nidd at a point now long submerged by Scar House Reservoir. It continued over the top of Dead Man's Hill to Horsehouse in Coverdale. Branches from this road led north to the various farms in the valley bottom.

However to bring materials for the construction of Angram Reservoir up from Pateley Bridge a road and light railway were built, the latter opening in 1907. The railway was dismantled in 1936 after the completion of Scar House Reservoir and its course all but obliterated by widening the adjoining road. The legacy is this private road, graded no steeper than 1 in 40, leading from Lofthouse into the upper reaches of the valley. It is the property of the Yorkshire Water Authority and is tarred throughout. A toll is payable by motorists, but cyclists may use it free of charge. To them it is a considerable benefit as it provides an excellent route into the head of the dale (and beyond into Coverdale), especially as the former road, deprived of its traffic, has been allowed to deteriorate beyond Middlesmoor and is a sorry state in places.

From Lofthouse the reservoir road runs up a sheltered part of the valley, which is very narrow and beautiful here. The river runs close by, but in dry weather what little water it is allowed to carry finds its way underground. Midway between Lofthouse and Scar House Dam the valley, and consequently the road, turns sharply to the left. Note the old railway tunnel cutting the bend.

> In the valley bottom, opposite the southern portal of the tunnel, is Manches-
> ter Hole, where daylight breaks into the underground main channel of the
> Nidd. The riverbed above is usually dry, and may be followed downstream
> to Goyden Pot, where the surface channel also branches underground. Ex-
> ploration a little way is possible, but not without a good light each.

The remainder of the way to the dam is steeper, but still a good cycling road. Just before the dam is the site of the temporary village of **Scar House** which sprung up to house and serve the workforce, several hundred strong. It was a self-contained community, with a church, cinema, shops etc.

Scar House Dam, 320m above sea level, is at a transition point. Below it the valley is well wooded and dotted with farms; above the hillsides are bare and featureless. One can continue up the valley road for $1^1/_2$ miles to the top dam (Angram), but there is little scenic value in the detour and the valley head is well seen on the way to Coverdale. A short distance up the Angram road, just past a white gate, the old road to Middlesmoor doubles back (see below).

The old road crossing from Scar House to Coverdale provides the cyclist with a useful link between the two valleys. Although some sections must be wheeled the track is quite clearly defined all the way so there is no risk of getting lost. The original track ran over the top of **Dead Man's Hill**, so named after the finding of bodies there, reputedly of travellers murdered by the landlady and daughter who ran the wayside inn at Lodge. This upper section of the track was later superseded by a new line passing to the west and crossing the watershed at a lower level. This latter section is still in excellent shape, and one of the finest 'green roads' in the Dales, though of no antiquity. Allow about $1^1/_4$ hours from Scar House Dam to Coverdale.

The right of way crosses Scar House Dam and bears left to run as a good cart track some way above the reservoir. In a mile or so it reaches the overgrown remains of Lodge, a sad reminder of the depopulation of

Gouthwaite Reservoir

the upper valley. A little further the track meets the original road from Middlesmoor, now severed by the reservoir. Leading up the hill is the one really poor section of the crossing, badly cut up, and requiring some hard work, especially near the top.

On reaching the level moor the going is easier, if still inclined to be boggy after wet weather. The condition of the track soon improves and after passing through a gate there is a long and well preserved section of road, with views opening up over Coverdale. At a bend the original route, a grassy trod over Dead Man's Hill itself, rejoins. Thereafter the track drops precipitously through a series of gates to the farm of Arkleside. After crossing the river the road along Coverdale is met, about 8 miles from Kettlewell and 10 miles from Leyburn. This is described in Route 30. The nearest village is **Horsehouse**, just down the valley, with a shop and an inn. In the opposite direction there is nowhere before Kettlewell.

The Nidd Valley High Level Route
The choice of routes up the valley beyond Lofthouse can be considered to be the water authority road first and the old road above Middlesmoor a poor second. For anyone who is prepared to exchange a smooth road for a grassy track there is a third way which the author has called the High Level Route. This 'contours' around the east and north of the

valley, at an elevation of about 400m, giving spectacular views over Nidderdale. It is more or less rideable, if bumpy in places, and clearly defined throughout. Its disadvantage is that, once on it, there are limited opportunities to cut it short without resorting to private roads or footpaths.

The track turns out of the Lofthouse-Masham road about $1^1/_2$ miles from Lofthouse and almost at the top of the hill. It runs alongside a wall for about half a mile to where the moor drops away precipitously into the deep gorge of the Nidd. The view over the valley is excellent, with the hilltop village of Middlesmoor prominent. The track runs north past a shooting lodge, in a mile reaching the junction of another track by an old guidestone, sadly defaced. Eastwards a good track leads over Pott Moor to the Masham road, while its western branch slants down to Bracken Ridge on the farm access road running along the valley at a lower level. This is linked to the water authority road at New Houses and at Limley.

The High Level Route sweeps round the crest of the moor, with views now of the distant reservoirs. After a long and very gradual descent some old coalshafts on the right are passed: hereabouts a bridleway, now untraceable in the heather, leads north by Little Haw into the headwaters of Colsterdale (see above). Continuing along the High Level Route a gate is reached, on the far side of which a recently made track is crossed at right angles. The bridleway keeps straight on to an old spoil heap, but thereafter is not only implausibly indirect, but by no means easy to follow. It is better to turn left at the gate (downhill), then to bear right onto an older track which drops to cross **Woo Gill**. All crossings higher up are dangerous. The way forward is soon clearly seen. Ignore a left branch — a promising start — which leads down to Low Woodale (footpath only). Keeping to the High Level Route the going is rather wet underfoot in places, but straightforward to Scar House. The site of the old reservoir construction camp stands out across the valley.

Those who have stuck it out as far as here fully deserve to return down the water authority road, which will take them effortlessly back to Lofthouse. Gluttons for punishment should seek out the old road, which doubles back out of the Angram road about 200m west of the dam (signposted Nidderdale Way). After a rough climb there is some good cycling over **In Moor** with a bumpy and just rideable descent to Middlesmoor.

Middlesmoor to Conistone (Wharfedale)

To give a foolproof description of this route would require more space than it deserves: it should not be taken without a companion, the two relevant Ordnance Survey maps and a compass. Allow 3 hours for this route which is 10 miles long. On some sections there is no defined path and in any case the Nidderdale side is not classed as a bridleway.

The key to the route is an access road which turns out of the In Moor road about half a mile north-west of Middlesmoor. In a mile or so turn left again and follow this road to its terminus at GR 053727. The objective then is to continue up the north side of **Straight Stean Beck**. The Ordnance Survey map shows a footpath near the river: this is not traceable, but there is a well defined path higher up the hillside which can be picked up about GR 045723. Once found this leads unmistakeably to the watershed fence and a small stile. Coming east make sure you cross here or you will be in all sorts of trouble. The path onwards soon expires but drops to pass an old shelter (a good landmark) and then a house by the Mossdale Beck. From here a good cart track leads over the hills to Conistone, the views improving all the way.

ROUTE 11
HARROGATE, KNARESBOROUGH and RIPON

Distances from Harrogate (miles): Via Ripley and A61: **Killinghall**
$2^1/_2$, **Ripley** $3^3/_4$, **Wormald Green** 7, **Ripon** $11^3/_4$.
Via Knaresborough: **Knaresborough** $3^1/_2$, **Copgrove** 8, **Bishop**
Monkton $10^3/_4$, **Ripon** $14^1/_4$.
Via Boroughbridge: **Knaresborough** $3^1/_2$, **Boroughbridge** $10^3/_4$,
Ripon $17^1/_2$.

INTRODUCTION

The three towns linked here — Harrogate, Knaresborough and Ripon
— are each important tourist centres in their own right. Harrogate is the
solidly Victorian spa town, Knaresborough an old market town attrac-
tively situated above the Nidd, and Ripon a compact cathedral city. All
three can be conveniently visited by cyclists travelling to or from the
Dales, particularly those also visiting York. For the latter some notes on
the approaches from that city are appended. The area to be covered is
all good cycling country and there are several byways which are worthy
of exploration but not described here.

Assuming a start from **Harrogate**, a look round the town is first
called for. Two hundred years ago Harrogate was an insignificant place
consisting of two separate villages, High and Low Harrogate, on the
open heath of Knaresborough Forest. Its mineral springs had already
been discovered and over the following years a fashionable spa developed. Nowadays the town has successfully widened its appeal and
capitalises on its position between York and the Dales as an excellent
tourist base and conference centre.

The buildings of the town recall the prosperous years of Victorian
and Edwardian England, but in a totally different way from its industrial

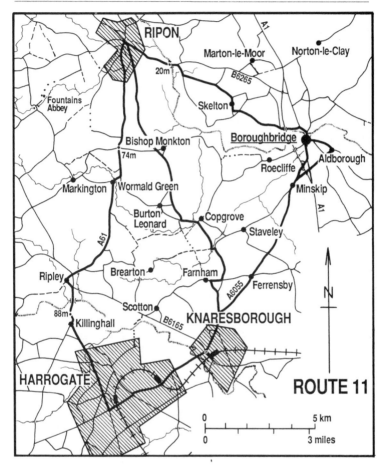

counterparts in the north. A unique feature of Harrogate is the Stray, a crescent of open park land almost encircling the town centre. When Knaresborough Forest was enclosed in 1770 the Stray was spared 'to be forever open and unenclosed'. Harrogate is very proud of its Stray and the floral decorations and gardens which have made the town a past winner of the 'Britain in Bloom' competition.

Harrogate holds a special place in cycling history for it was here in 1878 that a group of early enthusiasts founded the Bicycle Touring Club, soon to become the CTC. A commemorative plaque is situated in the gardens fronting the Prince of Wales Hotel on the Ripon road. Nearby are the former Royal Baths, the original Pump Room (now a museum) and other notable buildings of Low Harrogate. Harrogate's links with cycling are maintained by the town hosting the 'World of Wheels' cycle show and festival each summer.

Some distances from Harrogate (miles): **Harewood** $7^1/_2$, **Leeds** $15^1/_2$, **Pool** $8^1/_2$, **Bradford** $18^1/_2$, **Otley** $11^1/_4$ (Route 7), **Bolton Abbey** $16^1/_4$ (Route 8), **Pateley Bridge** 15 (Route 9), **Fountains Abbey** 10 (Route 13), **Wetherby** $9^1/_2$ (York 23).

> The A61 Leeds-Harrogate road is invariably busy, which detracts from its usefulness as an approach. Harewood House, the home of Lord Harewood, is open to the public in summer and offers a variety of attractions. The gardens are extensive and lead down to a lake.

THE ROUTE

Via Ripley and A61

This is a busy and, as far as Ripley, hilly road. Ripley is a most unordinary estate village lying on a short loop off the main road, which should be taken. For description of the village see Route 9. Beyond Ripley the road is less busy and crosses gently rolling country with no trying hills. The countryside is uninteresting but on the whole it is not a bad road. Markenfield Hall, a most unusual survival of a medieval fortified house, is occasionally open to the public. It lies about a mile west of the A61, from which it is just visible. The driveway is also a public bridleway, but its continuation north to Studley Roger cannot be recommended. For Ripon see Route 11.

Via Knaresborough

By turning left just south of Harrogate railway station the Knaresborough road is reached on the edge of the Stray. This is High Harrogate, one of the older parts of the town. The A59 on through Starbeck to Knaresborough is unremarkable, and invariably busy, with a long descent to the Nidd at the High Bridge. The road then rises to lead into Knaresborough High Street.

As a town **Knaresborough** has a long history and, though overtaken by its larger neighbour Harrogate as an administrative centre, is still a busy place. Passing along the main street you would not consider the town anything out of the ordinary, but turn off through the old market place to the castle and from the latter you will have a grand and surprise view over the River Nidd which runs in a deep gorge below the town. Across it runs the impressive railway viaduct.

Tourist Knaresborough can be considered to embrace the castle grounds and the river banks between the High and Low Bridges. There is a very narrow road along the east side of the river between the two bridges, but this gets very crowded with pedestrians in summer and so this part of the town is as well explored on foot. Rowing on the Nidd is a popular pastime and boats can be hired. Across the river a path runs through a park to the Dropping, or Petrifying Well, near the Low Bridge. Here a stream, trickling over an overhanging rock ledge, covers suspended articles with lime from the water. This takes several months and there is usually a macabre collection of visitors' knick-knacks, from teapots to teddy bears, undergoing the process.

The nearby Mother Shipton Inn commemorates the notorious witch and prophetess:

> 'Near to the famous Dropping Well
> She first drew breath, as records tell'

Little now remains of Knaresborough Castle except the ruined keep, but the grounds within the former outer walls have been laid out as an attractive public garden and various paths lead down to the riverbank walk. Knaresborough can also boast 'the oldest chemists shop in England' and a curious house carved out of the cliff face among its many and varied attractions.

Two miles south of the town, on the 'wrong' road to Wetherby, are Plompton Rocks, a smaller version of the more famous Brimham Rocks, near Pateley Bridge, but infinitely more accessible to the cyclist. The rocks overlook a pretty lake.

From Knaresborough traffic to Ripon is signposted via Ripley and the A61, but cyclists will find the following way much the preferable. Take the Boroughbridge road (A6055) for just over a mile, then the turn for **Farnham**. This is a pretty village, but lies just off route. The road, in fact, requires careful route finding as it skirts Copgrove on its way to Ripon. At **Bishop Monkton** Church turn right to include this very photogenic village. The countryside is undulating but without any troublesome hills and the road is a pleasant one for cycling. The turning off this road, through **Burton Leonard**, is the best cycling route from Knaresborough to Fountains Abbey ($11^1/_2$ miles).

Via Boroughbridge

This is a very roundabout route but with interest proportional to the extra distance. Beyond Knaresborough one can keep to unclassified roads by looping round via Farnham and Staveley but the main road holds no problems. This was the first road to be constructed by the remarkable 'Blind Jack of Knaresborough' who went on to lay out many of the turnpike roads in the area. Although losing his sight as a child John Metcalfe grew to be a man of many talents and could turn any venture to profit. So successful was his excursion into roadbuilding that he won contracts for roads throughout Yorkshire and neighbouring counties.

Boroughbridge was one of the great coaching centres before the railways came and grass grew over the Great North Road. Motor traffic brought business back to the town only for the bypass to take much of that away. After a period of decline it has perked up again. Just west of Boroughbridge are the Devil's Arrows, a trio of upright stones in a line straddling the Roecliffe road. Their origin and purpose are unknown.

Nearby **Aldborough** is a pretty village and the site of the Roman town of *Isurium*. It has a small museum of local finds. Until the Reform Act of 1832 Boroughbridge and Aldborough each returned two members to Parliament.

From Boroughbridge to Ripon the minor road via Skelton is to be preferred to the dull B6265. Just beyond Skelton is Newby Hall, a splendid Adam mansion with fine grounds and gardens.

Ripon is a small bustling town of obvious antiquity: it claims to have received its charter from Alfred the Great, no less, in 886. Its history as a centre of Christianity is even longer, for the Minster (since 1836 a cathedral) occupies the site of the church built by St Wilfred in 672.

The hub of Ripon is its crowded market square, dominated by a tall obelisk dating from 1781. On a corner of the square is the Wakeman's House, now a museum. The wakeman was responsible for the town watch, and a survival of these duties is the custom of sounding a horn each night in the square to set the watch.

Externally Ripon Minster is bulky rather than graceful. Internally it is noteworthy for the incongruities in design as the former twelfth-century building was extended and rebuilt. The fine carvings in the choir stalls date from about 1490, though later restored. From the nave steps lead down to the crypt, evidently part of St Wilfred's original church, which now houses the plate and regalia of the city. North of the Minster, in St Marygate, is the Prison and Police Museum, housed in the former gaol.

Some distances from Ripon (miles): **Fountains Abbey** 4 (Route 12), **Pateley Bridge** 12^1/$_2$ (Route 12), **Masham** 9^1/$_2$ (Route 29), **Northaller-ton** 17^1/$_2$, **Thirsk** 11^1/$_2$, **Easingwold** 16, **Malton** 35.

Approaches from York

Many cyclists will be visiting the Dales from York and so some notes on the approach roads may be useful. The principal roads from that city — the A59 and A64 — are best avoided (though the latter has cycle paths to Tadcaster), but this can be achieved quite easily at the cost of a few extra miles. The roads across the Vale of York are generally flat but dull. The rail service to Knaresborough, Harrogate or Weeton (for Otley) can also be utilised.

The key route from York is the B1224 to Wetherby ($13^1/_2$ miles) which turns out of the main Harrogate road $^3/_4$ mile from Micklegate Bar. Alternatively from the Youth Hostel at Clifton you can cross Clifton Bridge, at the A59 turn right then first left into Manor Drive which leads via a cycle 'gate' into the B1224 at Acomb.

From Wetherby roads lead up Wharfedale to Harewood (6 miles, Route 11) and Otley ($14^3/_4$ miles); to Harrogate ($9^1/_2$ miles) and Knaresborough ($7^1/_2$ miles). For **Knaresborough** a few miles can be saved by turning off the B1224 at Long Marston and continuing via Tockwith and Cowthorpe, crossing the A1 by a new flyover. This route passes the battlefield of Marston Moor (1644). It is also not a bad way to Boroughbridge and Ripon, turning off beyond Tockwith for Cattal. This avoids the A59 completely and is about 20 miles to Borough-bridge. Near **Great Ouseburn** a lane west of the B6265 continues as a good cart track to the A1, opposite the turning to Arkendale. This provides a most useful link to Fountains Abbey, Brimham Rocks, etc as it keeps you clear of the usual tourist traffic.

Other ways to **Boroughbridge** involve a start along the A19, turning off before Shipton through Newton and Linton-upon-Ouse. One route then crosses the river (small toll) to Great Ouseburn and the B6265. The other way is via Myton-on-Swale. The river bridge here provides a handy short cut for cyclists, as from it a mile of grassy track (bridleway) runs to Ellenthorpe, and the road on to Boroughbridge. By either of these routes Boroughbridge is about 18 miles from York, and Ripon 7 miles further.

ROUTE 12
RIPON to FOUNTAINS ABBEY, PATELEY BRIDGE and GRASSINGTON

Distances from Ripon (miles): **Fountains Abbey** 4, **Sawley** 5$^1/_2$, **Pateley Bridge** 12$^1/_2$, **Stump Cross** 17$^1/_4$ (Appletreewick 22$^1/_4$, Skipton 28$^3/_4$), **Hebden** 21$^1/_4$, **Grassington** 23.

INTRODUCTION

This road is very much against the grain of the land, and so by no means an easy one. There are 300m of ascent between Ripon and Pateley Bridge and 440m between there and Grassington. The principal attraction is, of course, Fountains Abbey, one of the premier ecclesiastical monuments in England, which can conveniently be included en route. The abbey, together with the adjacent grounds of Studley Royal Park, are now the property of the National Trust. Brimham Rocks lie just a few miles off the direct road and within easy reach. While at Pateley Bridge a run up Nidderdale (Route 10), one of the best cycling roads in the country, provides some 'soft' cycling before facing up to Greenhow Hill. On the latter stages of the journey it is perhaps better to foresake the rather dull direct road for the attractions of Wharfedale, by turning off for Appletreewick.

THE ROUTE

For **Ripon** see Route 11. Heading west from the town in 1$^1/_2$ miles is the turning for Studley Roger, from where a long straight drive leads through **Studley Royal Park** to the bottom lake. Here is the eastern entrance lodge to Fountains Abbey grounds, where tickets must be obtained, and where a detailed guidebook bought. Before passing through the gate the little Victorian church, which will have been observed from the drive, may be visited. The interior is very ornate, with much marble.

It is a mile from the eastern entrance lodge to the abbey, following the River Skell which has been canalised here between a series of lakes and ponds. Cyclists are permitted to wheel their machines along the principal path, a most valuable facility for those wishing to leave the grounds at the west gate. This concession is by courtesy only, and so cyclists should not abuse it by riding.

The walk up the valley is most beautiful, the landscape having been transformed by selective planting of trees and shrubs and adorned with various statues and follies, setting off the water. The centrepiece of the whole concept is, of course, the abbey itself, which comes into view on rounding a bend. There are sufficient remains for the visitor to get a full impression of what a powerful institution it once must have been. Founded by the Cistercians in the twelfth century it developed over the years, the tower being completed only shortly before the Dissolution. It is perhaps the best preserved of the major British abbeys and the beauty of situation is second to none.

After a thorough exploration of the abbey one can leave by the west gate. Do not overlook the fine Jacobean **Fountains Hall** nearby (separate admission charge). The road passing this west entrance is a minor one from Ripley to Masham, described in Route 13. If returning to Ripon (4 miles) the road north is followed to the B6265, but if con-

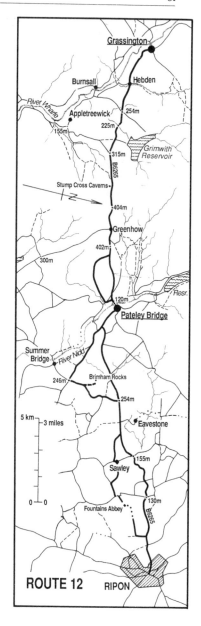

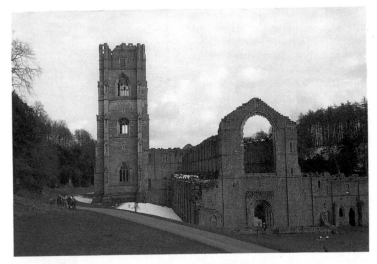

Fountains Abbey

tinuing west to Pateley Bridge or Brimham Rocks it is better to cross the Skell and take the first and second turnings to the right which climb to the little village of **Sawley**. Here turn left then right, this lane rising to meet the main road about 5 miles short of Pateley Bridge.

One is now on the moors about 200m up, but the toil continues for a mile or so until the foreground falls away to reveal the distant Nidd Valley. At this point a branch road south leads, in a few miles, to Brimham Rocks, described in Route 9.

Keeping on the B6265, one might at first imagine it is now all plain sailing down to Pateley Bridge. In fact after dipping to cross Fell Beck the road regains nearly all its lost height and then manages a few hiccoughs before the long descent into **Pateley Bridge**. For the town and vicinity see Route 9.

Pateley Bridge to Grassington

There are longer climbs in the Dales than that of **Greenhow Hill**, but few are nastier. There is a total rise of 290m in $1\frac{1}{2}$ miles, with three separate sections of 1 in 6, while the transition from the wooded valley of the Nidd to the bare moorland is a sad loss. There is an alternative road starting at **Bewerley**, looping round to the south, which may be used instead on the basis that if you are going to push up a hill it might as well be a quiet one. This, however, is even steeper in places and certainly cannot be recommended in the reverse direction.

Greenhow is one of the highest communities in Britain. It owes its existence to lead mining, and the old tips are still being reworked for other minerals. A mile or so further are the **Stump Cross Caverns**, a series of show caves in the underlying limestone. The distant prospect of Wharfedale provides some scenic interest, and the turning down to Appletreewick beckons one to greener pastures. Indeed there is a lot to be said for cutting down to the Wharfe and reaching Grassington via Appletreewick. The area is described in Route 1. The B6265 keeps to the less interesting high ground, with a steep drop to the awkward Dibbles Bridge, scene of some spectacular accidents. Upstream is the recently enlarged Grimwith Reservoir.

Hebden is a pleasantly situated village extending alongside the Hebden Beck. Cyclists rushing down one side of the dip to get up the other will have no more than a glance, noticing perhaps the old packhorse bridge north of the present one.

A track follows Hebden Beck northwards, petering out in a mile or so, but the agile may continue on the bridleway which fords the stream three times before turning west for Yarnbury and the road back down to Grassington.

Hebden to **Grassington** is a straightforward run of a couple of miles, the information centre being passed on the way into the latter. For Grassington see Route 1.

ROUTE 13

HARROGATE to FOUNTAINS ABBEY and MASHAM

Distances from Harrogate (miles): **Ripley** $3^3/_4$, **Markington** $7^3/_4$, **Fountains Abbey** 10, **Winksley** $12^3/_4$, **Kirkby Malzeard** $15^1/_4$, **Grewelthorpe** $16^3/_4$, **Masham** 20.

From Knaresborough, Fountains Abbey is best reached via Ripon or Burton Leonard (Route 11). The road from Knaresborough joining this route at Ripley ($4^1/_2$ miles) is rather dull.

INTRODUCTION

This route, branching from the main Ripon road at Ripley, traverses some attractive hill country between the Pennine moors and the Vale of York. It is also the road passing nearest to Fountains Abbey, the highspot of the journey, though the approach via Studley Royal is the more 'classical'.

The area west of Ripon is very beautiful, with steep wooded slopes, winding rivers and old villages. The soil is rich, the debris of glacial bulldozing in the dales to the north, through which the little Rivers Skell and Laver follow their strange deep channels. There is a wealth of lanes to explore, but hills must be expected. In addition there are some interesting bridleways, but these are all too often deep in mud.

THE ROUTE

The main road out of **Harrogate** is a series of ups and downs to Killinghall, after which the River Nidd is crossed. Turn aside for Ripley (Route 9). After following the Pateley Bridge road for half a mile the Fountains Abbey road turns off and uphill to run across a plateau of high ground. The road is straight for 2 miles and to relieve the monotony, as

84

Kirkby Malzeard

well as to escape the tourist traffic, the turning through Markington is suggested, which is hardly any further. After the two routes rejoin the road rises gradually, passing an old tower on the knoll, How Hill, to the left. This replaced an earlier chapel to St Michael.

Beyond the tower the road drops to the Skell Gorge and the western entrance to **Fountains Abbey**, which is just off to the right. The approach road passes Fountains Hall. If proceeding to Ripon cycles may be wheeled through the grounds to the eastern gate. For a brief description of the abbey see Route 12.

The road on to Masham is a trial of navigation. From the Skell bridge the road rises steeply, then levels out to skirt the village of Aldfield. It then goes more or less straight across the B6265 to drop to the River Laver, like the Skell in a deep wooded valley. If coming south turn left, not right, after the Laver Bridge; the signposted way via Aldfield is nearly a mile longer.

Beyond the Laver a long ascent (1 in 8) brings one to the hilltop village of Winksley, and a lovely run on via Winksley Banks to **Kirkby Malzeard**. The village centre lies off to the left, and should be included. The place was once of some importance, and the centre of administration of a large area between the Ure and the Nidd. Nothing now remains of the castle of the Mowbray family, but the name Vale of Mowbray is

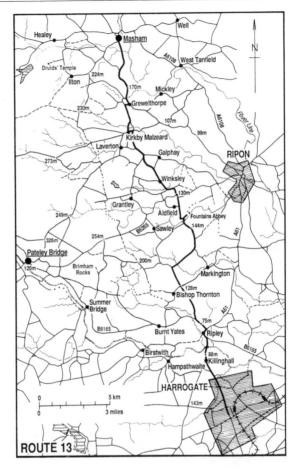

often given to the tract of land centred on Thirsk. Kirkby Malzeard was a market town and a great centre of packhorse roads, many of which have been incorporated into modern roads. Those west to Ramsgill (8 miles) and Lofthouse remain as metalled tracks in part, and provide some practical routes for cyclists who like to seek out the remote moorland ways.

From Pateley Bridge to Kirkby Malzeard is $8\frac{1}{2}$ miles. At the top of the main street in Pateley Bridge carry straight on up the extremely steep lane past the shell of the old church which provides a good viewpoint. This lane eventually emerges onto the moor, a dull crossing broken only by the dip into the little gorge of the Skell. This is unrecognisable as the graceful stream flowing past Fountains Abbey, only a few miles away. Southbound traffic to Pateley is signposted via the branch road to Wilsill which forks here to avoid the dangerous descent into the town. Beyond Skell Gill the moorland run continues for a couple of miles until a long and straightforward descent into the valley of the Laver. Watch out for the left turn a mile beyond the Drovers' Inn which leads to Laverton. There is an old guidestone at the junction, pointing to Masham, Pateley Bridge, Ripon — and Ripley! At Laverton turn left to enter Kirkby Malzeard from the west.

From Kirkby Malzeard there is a gradual ascent to **Grewelthorpe**, another neat village complete with green and duckpond. It was once famous for cream cheese.

Near Grewelthorpe, and reached by a footpath that turns out of the Masham road about a mile north of the village, is Hack Fall. Here the Ure pursues a turbulent course through a deep wooded gorge that scenically can hold its own with the Wharfe in Bolton Woods. The vicinity was once a popular tourist venue, but these days the paths have fallen into disrepair and the overgrown foliage obstructs any view of the river. Cyclists without a pair of stilts are advised to give it a miss.

Beyond Grewelthorpe the road surmounts a tough little hill, from the top of which the spire of Masham Church is prominent. The descending road provides a fine steeplechase into the town.

Masham is an interesting old place, not quite a town, but bigger than a village. Its vast market place suggests more lively days and the number of fine buildings, all in the pleasing local stone, are echoes of past importance.

Masham is now most famous for its brewery, home of the potent 'Old Peculier'. There is a new visitor centre. Masham is also host to the annual Traction Engine and Fairground Organ Rally in July.

West of Masham, between the Ure and the high moors, lies some beautiful and well wooded countryside not, alas, easy to explore by bicycle. One place of interest is the hilltop 'Druids' Temple', a folly based loosely on Stonehenge, built about 1800. It is about a mile north-west of Ilton.

Some distances from Masham (miles): **Lofthouse** $10^1/_2$ (Route 10), **Ellingstring Youth Hostel** 4, **Leyburn** 11 (Route 29), **Richmond** (direct) 15, **Bedale** $6^1/_2$, **Northallerton** $14^1/_2$, **Thirsk** 15, **Ripon** $9^1/_2$ (Route 29).

ROUTE 14
SKIPTON to SETTLE and MALHAM

Distances from Skipton (miles): **Gargrave** $4^1/_2$ (Malham $11^1/_2$),
Hellifield $9^1/_2$, **Long Preston** $11^1/_4$, **Settle** $15^1/_2$.

INTRODUCTION

The A65 from Skipton is a busy road, carrying a lot of traffic between
Yorkshire and the north-west of England and Scotland, including
holidaymakers bound for Morecambe, the Lake District and the Dales.
If it was not for this traffic it would be a lovely ride through varied
countryside, as for all its piecemeal improvements the road retains
some character, unlike so many other main roads which have been
upgraded and engineered to a monotonous regularity. So, providing it
is not a fine summer's weekend, the cyclist can confidently keep to this
road rather than be obliged to seek out alternatives, all of which are
either hilly or more roundabout. A bypass for Gargrave is in the
pipeline, and another proposed for Hellifield and Long Preston.

As this road passes within striking distance of Malham, many will
choose to turn off at Gargrave, to take the lovely lane following the Aire,
and reach Settle over the moors.

THE ROUTE

For **Skipton** see Route 2. There is a gradual climb out of the town, after
which the road drops to run near the Leeds and Liverpool canal, a
popular holiday waterway, to **Gargrave**. This is a pleasant village and
hospitable, for here the Pennine Way crosses our route. It is also situated
at the meeting of several good cycling byways and forms a popular
rendezvous. The canal skirts the edge of the village and once the wharfs
were busy with the transfer of produce. Now pleasure boats line its
banks.

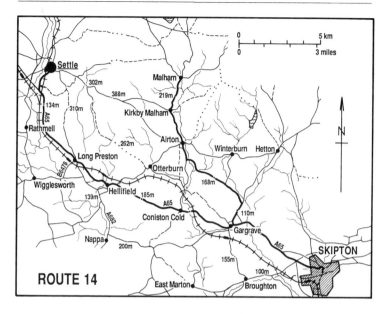

ROUTE 14

The route from Gargrave to Malham is $7^1/_2$ miles in total and is a cyclist's delight — off season at least. It can carry an incredible amount of tourist traffic for which it is ill suited. From Gargrave it first runs through the park-like grounds of Eshton Hall, then bobs up and down to Airton, a pretty village, as is Kirkby Malham a little further. From the road between them the distant Malham Cove may be glimpsed. Malham and its surroundings are described in Route 3.

For Settle the following quieter alternative to the A65 is suggested, should the latter be busy. This is via a minor road from Gargrave leading west to join the A682 near Nappa, south of Hellifield. This involves a few extra miles but no extra hillclimbing, despite a long gradual rise from Gargrave. The A65 is rejoined at Long Preston, or a further deviation via Wigglesworth may be taken, as described below.

From Gargrave the main A65 runs through fine rolling country with some pretty views around Coniston Cold before rising to cross Coniston Moor. Almost at the hilltop is the halfway milestone, $7^3/_4$ miles from both Skipton and Settle. The road summit is not only the highest point on this route, but the watershed between the Aire, flowing east, and the Ribble, flowing west. Congratulations — you have crossed the Pennines! The road drops to the railway village of **Hellifield**, which became a busy junction and operating centre following the opening of the Settle and Carlisle line. Now the ornate station, massive for present needs, is the only reminder of past importance.

One route from Hellifield to Settle is $8^1/_4$ miles via Wigglesworth. This is a series of byroads to avoid the A65, but increases the distance by a couple of miles. On entering Hellifield turn left at the Black Horse, then first right onto a narrow lane leading to the A682 from Gisburn. This is followed for a mile until a turning off to Wigglesworth ($3^1/_4$ miles from Hellifield). From Wigglesworth a minor road runs north through Rathmell to Settle, entered by the railway station. The gradients are easy throughout.

Beyond Hellifield the main road runs quickly to the attractive, if rather austere, stone-built village of **Long Preston**. This is the presumed site of a Roman fort, but no traces remain. The old road on to Settle did not keep to the valley bottom, but took a very direct course over Hunter Bark, rising to over 300m. This can still be easily followed by bicycle, only the middle section being untarred, but the descent into Settle is precipitous. As a through route it was superseded in 1753. Ordinary mortals will prefer to keep to the easily graded A65, which skirts the broad valley of the Ribble. After a stretch alongside the railway to the junction with the new bypass a slight rise brings one into the town of Settle.

Settle for most people is epitomised by its bustling market place, which even the new bypass is unlikely to quieten. Hospitable rather than handsome, the little town is most easily explored by that standard device, a short perambulation. After noting the quaint terrace of shops known as The Shambles, passing behind the Victorian Town Hall brings one to The Folly. This richly ornate building of 1675 was so-named because its cost drove the builder to bankruptcy. Opposite, in Chapel Street, is the Museum of North Craven Life. Taking the upper road at The Folly brings one to the older part of the town, and a milestone reminder that this was the old London road. Turning sharp left a lane runs below the limestone precipice of Castlebergh which overshadows the town. There is a winding path to the top, from which a good view over Lower Ribblesdale is obtained. Returning to the lane, a continuation along it brings one to Constitution Hill. This is fronted by a number of fine old buildings, and leads back to the market place.

Some distances from Settle (miles): **Burnley** 23, **Wigglesworth** 5, **Clitheroe** $16^1/_2$, **Slaidburn** $12^1/_2$ (Preston 34), **Clapham** 6 (Route 18), **Lancaster** 26, **Hawes** 22 (Route 16), **Malham** $6^1/_2$ (Route 3).

ROUTE 15
SETTLE to HALTON GILL
(LITTONDALE) and LANGSTROTHDALE

Distances from Settle (miles): **Stainforth** 2$^1/_2$, **Rainscar summit** 6$^1/_2$, **Halton Gill** 10, **Raisgill** (Langstrothdale) 12$^1/_2$. **Halton Gill to Arncliffe** 4$^1/_2$, **Kettlewell** 10, **Grassington** 12.

INTRODUCTION

This is a useful route from Settle to Wharfedale, reached by its pretty tributary, Littondale. The ambitious can also continue over the ridge separating Littondale from Langstrothdale, and then proceed to Wensleydale via Fleet Moss or Kidstones. These obscure byways and tracks are all routes of great antiquity which in olden days would have echoed to the teams of packhorses which supplied the dalesman with the necessities of life — salt, corn, wool for home spinning, and the latest gossip.

For cyclists the main bugbear of the road is the long broken rise beyond Stainforth to the summit at the watershed, a total rise of 260m. The reward is an easy run down the full length of Littondale.

THE ROUTE

From **Settle** to Stainforth — mainly uphill — see Route 16. Out of Stainforth the climb is very steep and does not ease up for 1$^1/_2$ miles to the hilltop above the farm of Sannet Hall. Here a track on the left comes up from Helwith Bridge, but this offers no saving in time from that part of Ribblesdale (see Route 17).

The road continues up a broad and uninteresting valley, Silverdale. Intermittently seen ahead is the prominent southern edge of Penyghent, and the rider will do well to remember that the watershed is not reached until the road has drawn square to it. The climb is one of fits and starts

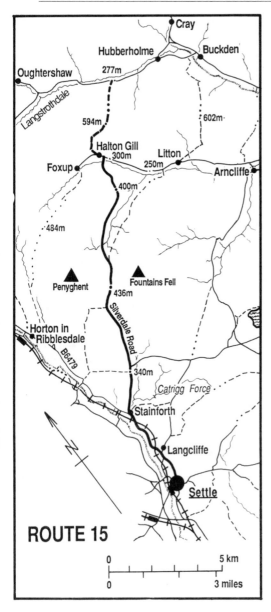

as far as **Dale Head**, where the Pennine Way crosses the cyclist's route. Just before the cattle grid a socketed stone on the right marks the site of Ufgil Cross, delimiting the border of the lands of Fountains Abbey, from which Fountains Fell owes its name. From here Penyghent looks its most impregnable, but it can easily be ascended in 40 minutes or so from the road. Cycles can be taken as far as the junction with the track down to Horton. It must be remembered that the track southeast from Dale Head, to the Malham road, is private. Fountains Fell, to the right of our road, presents an uninteresting outline.

Soon after Dale Head comes **Rainscar House**, with its sheltering band of trees, and the rather indeterminate summit, at a height of 436m. On the Littondale side the road drops only a little at first, passing the junction with a green road which cuts off the corner by heading straight to Litton. This has a poor surface on its lower, steeper, sections so is perhaps more practical in the reverse direction. The regular road gives you more chance to admire the scenery while still being quicker. After keeping high above the valley side it plummets at 1 in 6 down to Halton Gill. Coming south nearly all the spadework is done in the first mile.

The rider proceeding down Littondale, however tempted by the easy valley road, should first turn aside to explore the quaint old hamlet of **Halton Gill**, with its former church school and other old buildings. It was an important staging post in packhorse days. Now the nearest refreshments will be found at the inn or shop at **Litton**, a few miles down the valley. For a description of Littondale see Route 4.

Halton Gill to Raisgill (Langstrothdale)

This route is $2\frac{1}{2}$ miles long and 1 to $1\frac{1}{4}$ hours should be allowed for the crossing. It is the continuation of the above route from Horton, though thankfully not improved for motor traffic. This track (signposted Hawes, of all places) turns out of the Foxup road just west of Halton Gill, to soon double back up the hillside. It is a good cart track, rideable in the reverse direction, as far as the summit, from where there is an excellent all-round view. The descent to Langstrothdale commences over somewhat boggy grass but is clearly defined to where it meets the valley bottom road a little west of the few cottages which comprise Raisgill. This is situated in the most scenic part of Langstrothdale, the name given to the head dale of the Wharfe above Hubberholme. For the road to Buckden ($2\frac{1}{2}$ miles) or Hawes ($9\frac{1}{2}$ miles) see Route 5.

ROUTE 16
SETTLE to RIBBLEHEAD and DENTDALE

Distances from Settle (miles): **Stainforth** $2^1/_2$, **Horton** $6^1/_4$, **Selside** 9, **Ribblehead** (junction) $11^3/_4$, **Newby Head** (junction) $15^1/_2$ (Hawes 22), **Cowgill** $18^3/_4$, **Dent** $22^1/_2$, **Sedbergh** 28.

INTRODUCTION

This is a road through the spectacular scenery of the 'Three Peaks' — Penyghent, Ingleborough and Whernside — then dropping down to one of the least known of the Dales — Dentdale. A clear but not necessarily sunny day is required to get the best views: somehow Ribblehead viaduct looks its most impressive in overcast or misty conditions.

The lane from Giggleswick up the west side of Ribblesdale to Little Stainforth and Helwith Bridge is much more the pleasant cycling road, as the B6479 has been extensively rebuilt below Horton to cater for the quarry traffic. The byroad is secluded and quiet and one would not recognise the valley as being the same as that seen from the main road. The only advantages of the latter are the two villages that lie just off it — Langcliffe and Stainforth. Higher up the valley is bare and dependent on views of the Three Peaks for scenic effect.

The road up Ribblesdale is accompanied by the Settle and Carlisle railway line, which climbs at a steady 1 in 100 to Ribblehead: the road gradients are alas nothing like as regular! The line was a product of inter-railway rivalry. The Midland Railway wished to have its own Anglo-Scottish route, but the only way open to them lay through the wild hill country between the valleys of the Ribble and the Eden, tunnelling under Blea Moor and skirting Dentdale and Garsdale. The line was only constructed at a terrific cost, every section involving heavy engineering works, which have left a legacy of expensive maintenance. After the withdrawal of local trains in 1970 just a handful of expresses remained on the route. However in 1975 the Dales Rail service was introduced, special weekend trains calling at reopened stations, and this proved a turning point. As well as providing a useful service for those wishing to visit the Dales (including cyclists) the trains generated considerable interest in the line itself which is now appreciated as a major tourist attraction in its own right. This remarkable upturn in the line's usage, and a hard fought campaign, resulted in a reprieve from closure in 1989. The reopened stations are now served by daily trains and many are enjoying a better level of service than ever before.

In the days when rail travel ruled supreme most people's experience of Dentdale would be a brief one, a snatched glimpse of a green and sheltered valley, a lost Shangri-La, before the train would once more plunge into a tunnel. Nowadays most visitors make their way by road up Ribblesdale from the towns of West Yorkshire, but the valley still retains its feel of remoteness and old-worldness. The cyclist will find it a delight, with winding lanes begging to be ridden along.

THE ROUTE

Skipping for the moment the minor road from Giggleswick, the main road starts at **Settle** Bridge. This road can also be reached from Settle market place via Constitution Hill

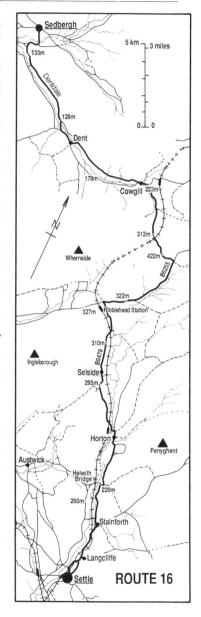

(ignore 'No Through Road' signs). The two roads unite just before **Langcliffe**, an interesting village worth turning aside to see. There is a pleasant green and a number of old buildings. A little north of the village, alongside the railway, is an old industrial limekiln which it is hoped can be restored as a tourist attraction. Continuing up the valley, which is at its narrowest here, a light climb brings one to **Stainforth** (a Youth Hostel is on left just before village). Stainforth is now bypassed, but again the visitor should turn aside.

> In olden times Stainforth was quite a focal point for packhorse roads. Many of these were later improved for wheeled traffic and now exist as motor roads, such as those up Ribblesdale or across to Littondale, while others have fallen into obscurity. This includes the east-west route via Mastiles Lane, Stainforth, Feizor and Austwick, an old route between York and Lancaster. This crossed the Ribble near Stainforth by a fine packhorse bridge which still survives. It lies on a narrow and unsignposted road turning out of the main Horton road just north of the village, running across to Little Stainforth and the minor road up the west side of the valley. Below the bridge are some deep pools and a little rocky gorge through which the water spills.
>
> A mile east of Stainforth is Catrigg Force (Route 17) a stiff uphill ride or walk. It can conveniently be included by cyclists en route to Malham Moor.

North of Stainforth there is a stiff but short hill to surmount before the valley broadens out considerably, with the familiar outline of Penyghent coming in to view. The scenery around Horton is impaired by the quarries which however provide much local employment. At Helwith Bridge the road up the valley is crossed by another once important route from Clapham across to Malham Moor, part of which is still a green road, Moor Lane (Route 17). The western branch from Helwith Bridge to Austwick and Clapham is a good cycling run once the quarries are passed.

The remainder of the run to **Horton** is easy with the road entering the village by the part-Norman church. Otherwise Horton has nothing of note, save being the 'official' starting and finishing point of the Three Peaks Walk, embracing the summits of Penyghent, Whernside and Ingleborough. The round, of about 22 miles, is now a very popular event at all times of the year, as the crowded car parks will testify. On the last Sunday of September is held the Three Peaks Cyclo-Cross Race, a sight to behold. The winning times of just over 3 hours (over a much longer route) are only slightly more than the best running times. Typical walking times are 8 to 10 hours. As well as being on the Three Peaks Walk, Horton lies on the Pennine Way and so is well provided with

Ribblehead viaduct

overnight accommodation.

At the north end of the village the road crosses to the west side of the valley, passing the station, and once under the railway climbs gradually for over a mile. Penyghent stands prominent across Ribblesdale. After dipping through the hamlet of Selside the road pursues an up and down course about 300m up until Ribblehead viaduct and the lonely road from Ingleton to Hawes are reached.

Ribblehead consists of a few railway and quarry cottages and the Station Hotel, a little to the left. Across the valley bottom strides the curving line of piers of the most famous structure on the Settle and Carlisle line. Elsewhere it would dominate the countryside; here, however, surrounded by the bleak gathering grounds of the Ribble and Yorkshire's Three Peaks the works of man and nature seem to hold each other in due respect. Ribblehead without its viaduct would be like Trafalgar Square without Nelson's Column.

The building of the viaduct was an enormous undertaking, expensive in money, time and lives. The men worked in terrible conditions, housed in temporary camps which sprung up on the moor. Sickness, rather than accidents, took the heaviest toll. The viaduct was extensively repaired following the line's reprieve.

From the road junction at Ribblehead the road northwards begins a steady climb for over 3 miles, past the former drovers' inn at Gearstones to just short of Newby Head, where the road to Dent turns left. After a short run across the moor, which here has its summit 422m up, the road begins a steep drop into Dentdale. Note the old stone pillars giving the distance to Sedbergh — a dozen of the sweetest and easiest miles the cyclist will ever enjoy. The road winds under Dent Head viaduct and crosses a little beck just above some falls. Opposite, right under the viaduct and isolated by it, is an old packhorse bridge.

From here the road descends more gradually, with the infant River Dee tumbling alongside over its limestone floor. In about half a mile Dentdale Youth Hostel is passed then, on the right, another mighty railway viaduct spans Arten Gill. Hereabouts stood the Dent 'marble' works, actually using a local limestone which could be dressed and polished until it acquired a dark marble-like sheen. The old road from Dentdale to Widdale ran up Arten Gill, but is now in a very poor state. Approaching the scattered hamlet of Cowgill the main valley road is joined by the hill road over from Garsdale Head.

The route from Cowgill to Garsdale Head is $4^1/_2$ miles long and one of the longest hills in the Dales, climbing 400m from Dent town. From the junction at the valley bottom the road is very steep as far as the railway bridge at Dent station. This, incidentally, is over 4 miles from Dent town. The gradient then eases to give a mile or so of steady plodding to a junction with a road contouring around the head of the valley. This is an old droving road — Gallowaygate — by which the herds of Scottish cattle were driven south to the markets of southern England. The unimproved part forms an excellent green road. Continuing north the road soon reaches its highest point, at 537m.

On these moors were various coal workings, giving this lane its other name, the Coal Road. It was first given a tarred surface in 1954, and by the state of the road on the steep descent to Garsdale Head it has not been repaired since. There are views over the valley to the distant Lakeland hills. Garsdale Head is 6 or 7 miles from Hawes and 12 miles from Kirkby Stephen (Route 24).

Garsdale may also be reached by an old track running north from Cowgill Bridge, which on the Dentdale side is in reasonable condition. The summit (392m) is very wet underfoot and the descent to Dandra Garth Farm in Garsdale badly cut up. If you must try it allow an hour.

Although visitors are now in Cumbria, until 1974 Dentdale and indeed the area around Sedbergh was a far-flung corner of Yorkshire's West Riding. This is reflected in the 'WR' posts on the approaches to the bridges, demarcating local and county responsibilities, as does the inscription on Cowgill Bridge.

Cowgill is situated in perhaps the prettiest section of the valley, which here makes a graceful curve. A narrow lane, crossing to the south side of the river, provides a slightly hillier road to Dent, but both this and the main road — if such a delightful lane could be so called — offer excellent cycling. The dale bottom is dotted with sturdy old farmsteads while the meadows and hedgerows abound with wild flowers.

Dent town will strike the visitor with its old-world appearance and then by its small size. Its population is now only a few hundred, but it was formerly more important than neighbouring Sedbergh. Improved communications elsewhere left Dent somewhat out on a limb but which indirectly has helped to retain many of its older features. Now, however, Dent can claim to be well and truly 'discovered ' and put firmly on the tourist map.

Even the cyclist will appreciate Dent's picturesque cobbled streets which meet at the fountain, a memorial in appropriate form to the pioneering geologist Adam Sedgewick, one of Dent's famous sons. A nearby path leads to the church, a solid, squat structure, perfectly in keeping with its surroundings. The chancel is floored in Dent 'marble'.

From Dent a road crosses into Barbondale, for Kirkby Lonsdale ($9^1/_2$ miles) and Ingleton (15 miles), described the reverse way in Route 21. Out of Dent a pretty alternative is by a track following Flounder Gill up to the 'Occupation Road' high above the valley. This is rideable to its meeting with the Barbondale road. Its eastern branch towards Deepdale peters out in a mudbath on the appropriately named Foul Moss. For the road via Deepdale to Ingleton ($10^1/_2$ miles), part of the Yorkshire Dales Cycleway, see Route 19.

From Dent to Sedbergh is $5^1/_2$ miles and here again there are two roads for part of the way. The 'main' road soon crosses to the north side of the valley, but there is an alternative way via Gawthrop. This is gated and the surface not nearly as good. If taken the river should be crossed at Rash Bridge, about $3^1/_2$ miles from Dent. By keeping south of the Dee one can continue around the foot of Holme Fell, still on an indifferently surfaced road, to join the A683 Sedbergh-Kirkby Lonsdale road (Route 21). One feature of Dentdale is that the level of scenery does not drop off as its lower end is approached: on the contrary the hills enclosing the neck of the valley beyond Rash are noticeably more rugged. One is now crossing a geological boundary — the Dent Fault — from the typical limestone-shale-gritstone structure which underlies most of the York-shire Dales to an area of older Silurian rocks which produce a more irregular topography. On rounding the valley mouth there is a good view of the town of Sedbergh before the road drops to cross the River Rawthey. On the way a loop road runs through the pretty hamlet of Millthrop.

For beauty of situation **Sedbergh** is almost unrivalled. It occupies a south-facing slope above the meeting of three rivers — the Rawthey, Clough and Dee — whose mingled waters enter the Lune just below the town. Hills embrace it on all sides, yet it is the centre of some excellent cycling.

The Howgill Fells, overlooking the town, were long neglected as a walking area, but have grown in popularity with visitors seeking a change from the more crowded peaks of the Lake District and the Dales. This increased tourism has in turn benefited Sedbergh. Although not especially interesting as a town there are a number of inns and cafes to welcome the traveller.

The town is mainly famous for its school, originally founded in the sixteenth century, which occupies a major role in its social and commercial life. Sedbergh was also an early centre of Quakerism. Although Sedbergh is now part of Cumbria, the area east of the Lune was incorporated into Yorkshire in 1131 and formed part of the West Riding until 1974. Like Dent, Sedbergh was famed for hand knitting and so has always had strong links with Kendal, the centre of that trade.

Some distances from Sedbergh (miles): **Kirkby Lonsdale** 11 (Route 21), **Kendal** 11 (Route 23), **Tebay** $9^{1}/_{2}$ (Route 25), **Kirkby Stephen** 14 (Route 25), **Hawes** $15^{3}/_{4}$ (Route 23).

ROUTE 17
SOME RIBBLESDALE BYWAYS

Routes covered: **Stainforth to Catrigg Force; Helwith Bridge to Sannet Hall** (Silverdale); **Horton to Halton Gill** (Littondale); **Horton to Beckermonds** (Langstrothdale); **Horton to Cam Fell and Fleet Moss** (for Hawes or Bainbridge); **Selside to Austwick or Clapham; Settle to Malham via Stockdale.**

INTRODUCTION

These routes are a collection of loose ends which for convenience are brought together here, rather than clutter up descriptions of the regular road routes. All these are ancient upland ways which have escaped improvement into modern motor roads, and offer much to the cyclist who does not mind a bumpy ride and quite a bit of pushing. Their common feature is the ease with which traffic is left behind and how remote these upland areas can be, even within a mile or so of familiar landmarks.

Of the tracks described, that from Horton to Beckermonds is the most useful, providing a link between Ribblesdale and the head of Wharfedale. Of the others the route from Selside to Austwick is perhaps the most interesting.

THE ROUTES

Stainforth to Catrigg Force

This is a popular walk from Stainforth by a quiet lane which continues up to meet the road from Settle to Malham Tarn. The cyclist can thus include the waterfall as a variation from the direct road via Langcliffe, or merely as a pedestrian excursion from Stainforth.

From the top of that village, and on the south side of the beck dividing it, a rough road turns steeply uphill, past somewhat superfluous speed derestriction signs. Higher up the lane the gradient eases and the surface improves for riding. When a gate is reached a signpost points down to the waterfall, within earshot, on the stream below. The fall and the dingle below it are charming.

If continuing uphill to meet the road from Settle, proceed beyond the gate where the track — unfenced and poorly defined — bears right to a gate on the skyline, thereafter becoming clearer and metalled to where it meets the road up from Settle more or less at its summit. If coming south on this road the turning is unsignposted, but is shortly after the cattle-grid at the hilltop beyond Cowside Farm.

Helwith Bridge to Sannet Hall (Silverdale)

Silverdale is the valley running north from Stainforth and traversed by the road to Halton Gill. Two tracks — old roughly-metalled roads — lead up from Helwith Bridge to meet it.

The southern arm is **Moor Head Lane**, running east to Sannet Hall. This forms part of the old east-west monastic way, of which Mastiles Lane is the best known section. Starting from the B6479 the lower stages are steep and worse for wear, but by the summit (360m) it is much better, improving all the way to Sannet Hall. If heading west the road round via Stainforth is preferable.

The other branch from Helwith Bridge is via Dale Head, the track turning out of Moor Head Lane to head towards the distant peak of Penyghent. This is **Long Lane**, and 'long' it is, with 2 miles of steady ascent, uncomfortably slow going up and uncomfortably fast coming down. The views over Ribblesdale are the only compensation. The track finally drops to meet the Pennine Way en route for Penyghent, the summit of which may be reached by a walk of half an hour or so. Turning east, the track, which is wet in places, continues past Dale Head to the Stainforth-Halton Gill road about half a mile south of its summit. For continuation to Littondale see Route 15.

Horton to Halton Gill (Littondale)

Here is a route crossing a dreary watershed, devoid of interest beyond Hull Pot. Allow about 2 hours from Horton to Halton Gill (about 6 miles). The route starts from the post office at Horton, and is signposted the Pennine Way. It is a good solidly-metalled track, but rather uneven in surface so little of the initial uphill stages can be ridden. Where the Pennine Way turns right in $1^1/_2$ miles various tracks lead straight on, the lowest of which bring one to (and if not careful into) **Hull Pot**. This is 20m deep and spans the entire valley bottom. Into this cleft drop the waters of a beck which then continues underground.

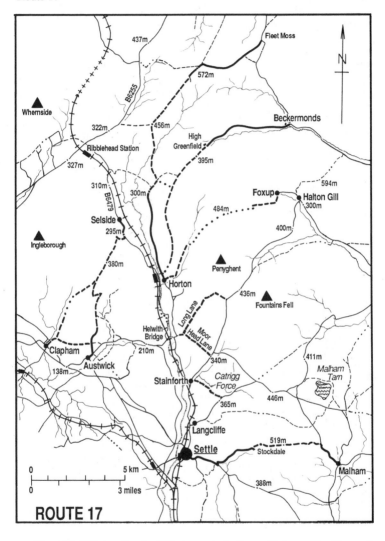

ROUTE 17

From Hull Pot cut back a little to a gate in the wall alongside. Beyond this the track, now just an uneven grassy trod, climbs alongside a stream to a corner of a wall where it is crossed by the Three Peaks Path from Penyghent to Ribblehead. Keeping to the wall on the right the route runs north-east across rough waterlogged ground and fording innumerable rivulets. The highest point is 485m. At Swarth Gill Gate it loses the accompanying wall, but the route is then waymarked and in any case distinct. This part of the crossing is much drier, gritstone having given way to limestone, and in places rideable. A short drop leads to a cart track at a slightly lower level which contours for $^3/_4$ mile before descending to Foxup through a series of gates. This is at the end of the tarred road up Littondale, described in Route 4. The nearest inn and shop are at Litton, 3 miles down valley. At Halton Gill Route 15 from Settle is crossed.

Horton to Beckermonds (Langstrothdale)

This is a handy link, following what was anciently a packhorse way from Ribblesdale to Langstrothdale and then via Kidstones to Wensley-dale and Richmond. Allow about $1^1/_2$ hours from Horton to Becker-monds (8 miles), but some time can be saved by taking the lane to Old Ing and then the forestry road described below.

From the north end of Horton village turn right at the Crown Inn onto the Pennine Way, a steeply-rising cart track. The surface is variable but most can be ridden. In a mile are **Sell Gill Holes**, some deep 'pots' either side of the track, which soon levels out at about the 380m contour. Two and a half miles from Horton the Pennine Way diverges to the left, but the track leads straight forward, in half a mile reaching a gate on the boundary of Greenfield Forest. Alongside is another gate on the forestry road leading up from Old Ing. This link up from Old Ing is private and the gates sometimes locked. Provided nobody objects to its use this provides a much easier way to or from Horton, employing the tarred road between Horton and High Birkwith.

The way forward through the plantation is the continuation of the bridleway which has been followed from Horton. It has a good surface, generally of limestone. Branches turn left and right, but the way is forward and unmistakable. This part of the valley is relatively unattrac-tive and with its bare rolling hills flanked by young plantations has a distinctly Scottish air. Ingleborough appearing behind over the water-shed is a reminder that the visitor is still in Yorkshire. At High Greenfield a tarred road starts, leading down to **Beckermonds** 3 miles and many gates away.

Horton to Cam Fell and Fleet Moss (for Hawes or Bainbridge)

Distances from Horton (miles): **High Birkwith** $2^3/_4$, **Ling Gill Bridge** $4^1/_2$, **Cam End** $5^1/_2$, **junction with Buckden-Hawes road** $10^1/_4$, **Hawes** 14 or **Bainbridge** 16.

This tour is an exploration of some old packhorse routes, including a section of the Roman road over Cam Fell. There is the choice of continuing on this and reaching Wensleydale at Bainbridge, but on reaching the Hawes road with its 300m descent beckoning most will call it a day and opt for the quick way down.

Jeffrey's Map of Yorkshire (1775) shows this as the only road north from Horton, and omits the present one via Selside. At that time the road down Widdale to Hawes had not been built, so the Cam High Road was taken by all traffic (including wheeled) from Ingleton to Wensleydale.

From the bridge at Horton a lane runs due north to terminate at the farm of **High Birkwith**. This was an inn in the old packhorse days. The road continues as a broad gravel-surfaced track up the hill to **Old Ing**, where a narrow lane bears left beyond a gate. This is also followed by the Pennine Way and is an easily-rideable metalled lane, though muddy in parts. A mile beyond Old Ing a pretty limestone gorge appears on the left; this is **Ling Gill** which is presently crossed by a fine old bridge. A worn inscription notes that it was repaired at the expense of the West Riding in 1765 — an indication of the former importance of the route which is being followed. The bridge and its environs form a tempting spot to linger at, for onward lie only the bleak gritstone moors.

The track beyond is still well defined, but poorly drained in places as it climbs to the ridge ahead. Here, at Cam End, it meets the Roman road which leaves the B6255 a mile to the west. This provides an alternative route from Horton or Ribblehead and is the quickest way off the moor in bad weather. The track onward is clear and unmistakable, but in several places badly cut up. Below is the curving double-ended valley draining westward to the Ribble and eastward to the Wharfe. The track gradually improves and becomes tarred at the junction with the access road to the remote Cam Houses.

Hereon it is an excellent hilltop run, passing in $^3/_4$ mile the junction with the Pennine Way which follows another former packhorse route on its way to Hawes. This, incidentally, is an excellent green road, particularly in its upper stages. A little further the motor road over **Fleet Moss** is joined, with its superb 4-mile run down to Hawes.

The continuation of the Roman road, which carries straight on to Bainbridge, is rideable and provides an opportunity to visit Semer Water on the way. This section of the road is described in Route 5.

Selside to Austwick and Clapham

This old packhorse route runs unenclosed from Selside, mid-way between Ribblehead and Horton, south to Clapham or Austwick. It offers some spectacular views across to Penyghent and of the limestone plateau of Sulber on the eastern flanks of Ingleborough. There are some problems of route finding, trivial in clear weather, but the lack of landmarks near to hand is unnerving in mist. Most of the upland sections of the track are easily graded and quite rideable; even so allow about a good hour from Selside to Austwick, $1\frac{1}{2}$ hours to Clapham. The highest point reached is 386m.

The bridleway turns out of the B6479 about $\frac{3}{4}$ mile south of the hamlet of Selside, just over the brow of a nasty little hill. There is a signpost to Clapham. Follow signs for Borrins and Gill Garth, but when the farms come into view on the right keep straight on (ie west), across a stream to a gate. Beyond this turn left, through another gate. This leads onto a vast gently-rising pasture, the track rather indistinct but keeping parallel to a wall about 100m to the right. This wall is the best guide as it sets the direction for the next 2 miles. A gate is passed through in a cross wall beyond which the track is clearer, following a terrace in the limestone and soon crossing the Three Peaks Path leading down from Ingleborough to Horton. Keeping straight on another gate is reached, just where the grassy plateau on the left drops away to reveal a vast limestone pavement. Below is the green and inviting valley containing Wharfe and Austwick. Beyond the gate the track, stony and well defined, continues among more limestone terraces for about $\frac{3}{4}$ mile to where a small pile of stones marks the division of the tracks to Clapham and the first track to Austwick.

The direct track to Clapham continues over the grassy moor, and is soon crossed by a second track down into Crummackdale. Here keep slightly right, skirting a low limestone outcrop and soon after the track begins to drop into the valley above Clapham. It works its way down to a gate in a wall, then drops steeply to another gate at the head of a lane leading down to the village. Just across the valley is the deep recess of Trow Gill (Route 18), easily accessible on foot. The way down to Clapham is by the appropriately named Long Lane, much of it too rough for riding.

For **Austwick**, and the better way to Clapham, bear left at the pile of stones mentioned above. The track soon winds down into Crummackdale. The lower stages, over smooth turf, are a little hard to trace if coming north, and confusion is caused by there being more than one branch. On reaching **Crummack** the grounds of the farm are not entered, but the track follows a wall south to meet the road end. This provides excellent cycling right down to Austwick, with a branch track (rather muddy) to Wharfe for those returning to Ribblesdale.

At the hill-brow above Austwick a footpath west from the road leads in 5 minutes to one of the geological showpieces of the Dales, the Norber Erratics. Here the hillside, obviously of limestone, is littered with dark, angular boulders of earlier origin, borne here by glacial action. Some of the best examples, a little higher up, occupy curious pedestals of limestone, showing how the surrounding rock has been worn away. There are excellent views.

Continuing down to Austwick, just before the village (entered by Townhead Lane) **Thwaite Lane**, another green road, is crossed. This leads in $1^1/_2$ miles to **Clapham** and is rideable throughout, save for the final descent, which is partly in tunnel under the grounds of Ingleborough Hall. For Clapham see Route 18.

Settle to Malham via Stockdale (6 miles, $1^1/_2$ hours)

This is a fine upland crossing and quite practicable throughout, being on distinct grass or stony tracks with no route finding problems. Scenically it is superior to the road routes.

From Settle the Kirkby Malham road is followed for $1^1/_2$ miles (all uphill) to where a lane on the left is taken. This is tarred to Stockdale Farm, just before which a cart track bears left through a gate. The initial stages are a little muddy and wet, but the track soon climbs out of the valley in splendid style to the moorland summit (519m), reached at the second gate. A grassy track descends slightly to the next gate passing an old mine spoil heap. Conspicuous on the wall to the left is Nappa Cross, an ancient guidepost (restored). Beyond it is a glimpse of Malham Tarn. Keeping straight on, the track descends over grass to become metalled for the final steep drop to join the road up from Malham. This is met opposite the top of the Cove to which, however, there is no direct path. Watch out for pedestrians on the long road descent into Malham village.

ROUTE 18

SETTLE to INGLETON and KIRKBY LONSDALE

Distances from Settle (miles): **Austwick** $4^3/_4$, **Clapham** $6^3/_4$, **Ingleton** 11, **Cowan Bridge** $15^1/_2$ (Casterton 18), **Devil's Bridge** $17^1/_4$, **Kirkby Lonsdale** $17^3/_4$.

INTRODUCTION

This is a reasonable enough road, save for one rather dull section between Clapham and Ingleton. Both these villages lie off the main A65 road, as does Austwick, and so until the other side of Ingleton the A65 can be avoided almost completely. The Yorkshire Dales Cycleway keeps entirely to minor roads, looping round via Giggleswick and Clapham stations through rather empty countryside: although the Austwick route involves a little bit of main road it is 2 miles shorter and the more interesting. Both Clapham and Ingleton are gateways to scenic side-valleys while Kirkby Lonsdale is one of the least spoilt minor towns of England.

THE ROUTE

For **Settle** see Route 14. After crossing Settle Bridge it is worth turning aside a little way down into **Giggleswick** village, which contains a number of fine old cottages and pretty nooks. The old Kendal road climbs at 1 in 6 past the famous school, but surprisingly its summit is lower than Buckhaw Brow, on the former A65. The main road can then be rejoined via Lawkland, which has a splendid old hall.

The main road from Settle runs below the white limestone cliffs of **Giggleswick Scar**. This section of road is winding and narrow and was rather uncomfortable for cycling before the bypass was built. By the roadside, in the last dip before the long rise to Buckhaw Brow, is the

Ebbing and Flowing Well. This has a reputation for filling and emptying of its own accord and the Victorians, whose fascination for plumbing knew no bounds, would sit and watch it for hours. These days, with traffic whizzing by, the spot is not one to linger at.

The climb to **Buckhaw Brow**, long visible ahead, must now be faced. From the well the road rises 75m, which is insignificant by Dales' standards but still quite a pull. Looking back from the summit one gets a good impression of the Craven Fault, separating the high limestone country to the north from the lower gritstone and shales to the south.

There are some interesting bridleways in the area. Above Austwick is Thwaite Lane, running from near Wharfe to Clapham, which provides a reasonable ride, and avoids a bit of main road. The road up Crummackdale is a good one, and passes near the famous Norber Erratics. These and the way over from Selside in Ribblesdale are described in Route 17. One other byway which must be mentioned is that which leads from Feizor, a delightfully situated hamlet, over to the Helwith Bridge-Austwick road. It is a through route to nowhere, but all the more enjoyable. By contrast the direct bridleways from Feizor to Austwick are impassably muddy.

After a corresponding drop on the western side of Buckhaw Brow, on which the bypass is met, the A65

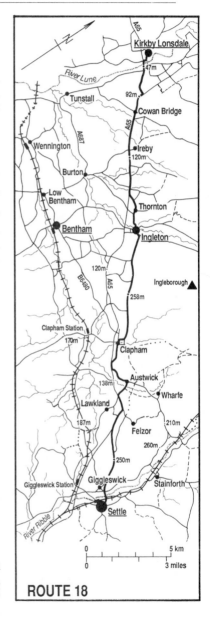

ROUTE 18

jinks its way to Clapham. Cyclists will probably choose the slightly
longer loop road via Austwick, a well-built and attractive village. **Austwick** lies in a pleasant side valley, which provides a link between
Clapham and Ribblesdale. A lovely winding lane runs up this valley,
but what a shock when the summit is reached, to be followed by a dismal
run past the quarries! Austwick to Horton is $5^1/_2$ miles. Between Austwick and Clapham the main road is only rejoined for a quarter of a mile
(lightly loaded cyclists can, of course, use Thwaite Lane, mentioned
above. Turn up Townhead Lane, Austwick, then left at the hilltop).

The former A65 never did **Clapham** justice, as to see it properly you
need to take the lane up to the church and then return down the far side
of Clapham Beck, which pursues a shady course through the middle of
the village. The National Park Information Centre should be an automatic place of call.

Attractive though the village is, its main appeal is the hidden valley
of **Clapdale**, just above it. This is best explored afoot by taking the
Reginald Farrer Nature Trail. Alternatively a bicycle could be taken on
the bridleway via Clapdale Farm. The Nature Trail is a broad and easy
footpath leading through delightful and varied scenery. A long mile
from the village, it reaches **Ingleborough Cave**, a show cave with
conducted tours. At the head of Clapdale is Trow Gill, a pretty gorge in
the limestone. The path onwards over the moors is one of the main
routes to Ingleborough and passes Gaping Gill, more than 100m deep.
Over Bank Holiday weekends visitors can enjoy the doubtful thrill of
a trip down by winch.

Some distances from Clapham (miles): **Slaidburn** 12, **Lancaster**
20, **Carnforth** 18, **Horton in Ribblesdale** $7^1/_2$.
For bridleway to Selside see Route 17.

Beyond Clapham there is a choice of roads to **Ingleton**. The better
one, followed by the Yorkshire Dales Cycleway, leads from the top of
the village and is the harder going, but avoids all the traffic, which can
be seen scurrying along the A65 below. This latter length of road was
built in 1831 to bypass the hills on the old road through Ingleton, and
is still noticeably straighter than adjoining parts of the A65. Clapham
had to wait for another 142 years for its bypass!

The A65 skirts Ingleton to the south, but the village is worth a look
even if its main tourist attraction, the falls, are not to be visited. These
require a couple of hours at least. Ingleton has an information centre and
various cafes and shops geared to the tourist. A couple of miles up the
Hawes road are the White Scar show caves.

Thornton Force

At Ingleton the falls of the Waterfalls Walk are situated on the two rivers, the Doe and Twiss, which unite just below the bridges at Ingleton. By walking up the western valley and returning via the eastern a circular walk of 4 to 5 miles (2 to 3 hours) can be enjoyed. The path starts just across the bridges and a small toll is payable towards the upkeep of the path, which is well maintained with steps at all awkward points. The whole route is clearly signposted.

The first mile or so, up the Swilla Glen, is rather enclosed, following the limestone gorge of the river. The path then reaches the long series of cascades known as Pecca Falls. After much climbing the path opens out into a typical limestone valley, with a beautiful approach to Thornton Force, the finest single fall on the circuit. Here the water drops 12m over a limestone shelf onto a bed of far-older rocks. It is possible to walk behind the fall. Above it the path winds up to Twistleton Lane, a splendid green lane linking the roads up Kingsdale and Chapel Dale.

Passing Beezley Farm the river is met at Beezley Falls, below which it has worn its way through transverse beds of rock to produce a most impressive gorge. There are a whole series of falls and deep pools after which the path runs below some old mine workings to re-enter the village by a lane.

Some distances from Ingleton (miles): **Bentham Station** 4, **Slaidburn** $15^1/_2$, **Lancaster** 18, **Carnforth** 15, **Dent** $10^1/_2$ (Route 19), **Hawes** $16^1/_2$ (Route 20).

West of Ingleton the best road for Kirkby Lonsdale, by reason of it postponing a return to the A65, is that dropping down by the railway viaduct then rising again to **Thornton in Lonsdale**. Here bear left at the church, not before. Traffic on the A65 is lighter beyond the Lancaster turn and the Kirkby Lonsdale road winds through pleasant rolling countryside. At **Cowan Bridge** was the school attended by Charlotte Brontë and later described in *Jane Eyre*. A little further, a side turning leads to Casterton, on the road up the Lune valley, but it is worth travelling the few extra miles to include Kirkby Lonsdale. In particular one should not miss the **Devil's Bridge**, just upstream from the Lune Bridge on the A65, and so-called from its unknown origin and mighty span. The rocky riverbed and grassy banks make this a popular spot for a picnic, or even a swim, and there is a strategically placed snack bar.

The town of **Kirkby Lonsdale** is set some way above the river and off the main traffic routes. Those who take the trouble to visit it will not be disappointed, for it is an unspoilt stone-built town of quaint nooks and curious street names, centring on a little square. There is a famous view over Lunesdale from the churchyard.

Kirkby Lonsdale to Kendal
As this is the main link from West Yorkshire to the Lake District some notes on the cycling routes may not be out of place. (See also the author's *Cycling in the Lake District,* MPC, 1984.) The direct road to **Kendal** ($11^3/_4$ miles), the B6254, involves a long gradual climb from Kirkby Lonsdale, then a series of ups and downs for the remainder of the way. The easier cycling road to Kendal, a mile longer, is to keep to the A65 through Lupton, Crooklands and Endmoor. North of the M6/A591 junction this road is fairly quiet. Via Crooklands and Heversham one can get to Newby Bridge (22 miles) or Bowness (22 miles).

The other approach to the Lakes is by road to Arnside, then by train across the Kent estuary to Grange-over-Sands. From Grange there are a number of good cycling roads into the heart of the Lake District. The easiest way to Arnside (13 miles) is via Crooklands and Milnthorpe.

Some distances from Kirkby Lonsdale (miles): **Slaidburn** 20, **Lancaster** 17, **Carnforth** 11, **Morecambe** 17, **Sedbergh** 11 (Route 21) **and Dent** 10 (Route 21), **Bentham** $8^1/_2$.

ROUTE 19

INGLETON to DENT VIA KINGSDALE AND DEEPDALE

Distances from Ingleton (miles): **Thornton in Lonsdale** $^3/_4$, **Deepdale Hause** $6^3/_4$, **Dent** $10^1/_2$ (Sedbergh 16). **Ingleton to Dent via Ribblehead** (Routes 20 and 16) is 17 miles. **Via Casterton** (Routes 18 and 21) **Dent** is 15 miles, **Sedbergh** $16^1/_2$.

INTRODUCTION

This route is the shortest way from Ingleton to Dentdale, and part of the Yorkshire Dales Cycleway. It involves more hillclimbing than the alternatives — via Ribblehead (which gives you a run down the full length of Dentdale), or via Barbondale (which is a longer but prettier run). Northbound the level valley of Kingsdale breaks the climbing neatly in two; southbound there is the massive haul to Deepdale Hause, an unrelieved rise of 335m out of Dentdale. The road is one of the very few in the Dales still to retain gates, which though not convenient for cyclists does deter a few motorists.

If proceeding on the Cycleway, which from Dent runs up the valley, the traveller should first make the diversion to Sedbergh — only half an hour away — and as pretty a ride as could be wished. Similarly those heading down the valley should turn off before Dent, ride up the dale at least as far as Cowgill, then return down the road on the far side of the river. Dentdale is too good to rush through, so make the most of it!

THE ROUTE

After the climb from the bridge at **Ingleton** the road bears right at **Thornton in Lonsdale**, a little village still retaining its old stocks by the church. There follows a long ascent — not too steep — which brings one out overlooking Kingsdale, a high upland valley in limestone country. Ingleborough presents a fine profile across the next valley.

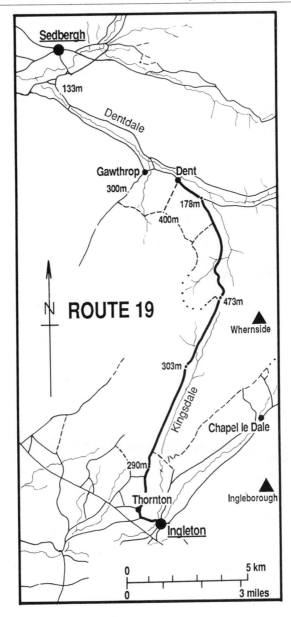

A green lane on the right runs below Twistleton Scar, providing an alternative route up from Ingleton for the mildly adventurous. It passes near Thornton Force (Route 18), but strictly speaking the path down to this splendid fall is part of the 'Waterfalls Walk' for which a charge is made.

The run onward along **Kingsdale** is easy. The river bed, over limestone, is often dry as the water is carried underground. About half a mile before the farm at Kingsdale Head is **Yordas Cave**, in a wooded dingle just to the left of the road. Its entrance is unimpressive, but this soon opens out into a large cavern. Yordas Cave is on private land and so should not be explored without permission.

Beyond Kingsdale Head the road climbs steeply. The long whaleback hill on the right is **Whernside**, no less, and from shortly before the top of the pass a footpath, following first a fence and then a wall, climbs to the summit (30 to 40 minutes). This path is only remarkable as being the easiest way up Whernside, and is for clear weather only. On reaching the road summit (Deepdale Hause, 473m) the view north extends over Dentdale to the shapely Howgill Fells beyond Sedbergh.

The track doubling back just beyond Deepdale Hause, and holding out the promise of fine views, does not live up to expectations and soon deteriorates into a linear mudbath. This upland enclosure road represents one extreme of Dales cycling, the leafy lanes of the valley bottom the other.

The descent into **Deepdale** is precipitous; in addition there are two gates to watch out for, one at the foot of a 1 in 4 gradient! At the bottom of this steepest section there is a pretty roadside waterfall on Gastack Beck. Thereafter the gradients are more manageable down to **Dent**. For Dent see Route 16. The road then down the valley is described in Route 16, the road up the valley and over to Hawes is described in Route 23.

NB coming from Dent the direct Ingleton road — not signposted — passes to the *right* of the George & Dragon.

ROUTE 20
INGLETON to RIBBLEHEAD and HAWES

Distances from Ingleton (miles): **Chapel le Dale** 4, **Ribblehead** (junction) 6¹/₄, **Newby Head** (junction) 10 (Dent 17), **Hawes** 16¹/₂.

INTRODUCTION

This direct route across the Dales is generally of little interest. The most scenic section is that between Ingleton and Ribblehead, with good views of the 'Three Peaks'. There is a choice of road as far as Chapel le Dale, both involving steep climbs out of Ingleton: that on the north side of the valley via Beezley is the more pleasant, the main road ranks a little easier and also passes the White Scar Caves. There is also a good 'rough-stuff' route — Kirkby Gate, over Scales Moor.

Despite the altitude of much of the road there is no climb worse than the initial one out of Ingleton. The highest point on the route (437m) is reached at Newby Head, but there is an intermediate watershed to cross between Chapel le Dale and Ribblehead. There is a notorious wind-gap between Ingleborough and Whernside, exposed to the prevailing south-west winds, which often makes this road very hard going if coming from Hawes.

THE ROUTE

There is a very steep climb out of **Ingleton** for a mile or so before the road emerges into a relatively flat upper valley and typical limestone country. On the right are the White Scar Caves, which are open to the public daily in summer.

A couple of miles of level road lead to the foot of a hill, where the alternative road from Ingleton comes in. A short way down this is the hamlet of **Chapel le Dale**, with its beautifully-situated little church. It contains a memorial to the many workers and members of their families who died during the construction of the Settle and Carlisle railway, just over the hill. Not far from the church is Weathercote Cave, which contains an underground waterfall, but to which there is now no public access.

The lane climbing just above the church leads up to a line of farms along the foot of Whernside and may be followed, as a bridleway, under the railway viaduct to regain the road at the Horton turn.

Beyond Chapel le Dale the road climbs past the Hill Inn — a comfortable hostelry familiar to Three Peakers — and descends into the moorland basin that forms the gathering grounds of the River Ribble. The views are on a grand scale, with Ingleborough, Whernside and Penyghent in sight, together with the famous curving railway viaduct that fits in so well with its sombre surroundings.

There is no village at **Ribblehead**, just a station (or half a one: only southbound trains stop here), the Station Inn, some quarries and one or two cottages, but the spot is a popular rendezvous for hikers and railway enthusiasts. There is usually a refreshment van at the road junction which provides the last opportunity for a snack before Hawes, still 10 miles off. For the road up from Settle and Horton see Route 16.

Beyond Ribblehead the

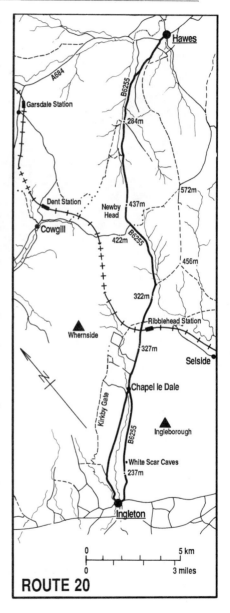

ROUTE 20

Chapel le Dale

road rises gradually but persistently, with good views back towards Ingleborough. In a mile or so the road passes the one-time inn at **Gearstones**, which catered for the cattle-droving trade. In the days before the railways great herds of cattle passed this way from Scotland to feed the burgeoning populations of London and other cities. These herds would be wintered on local farms before continuing their journey south, and Gearstones was one of the various meeting and trading points in the Dales. It also had a weekly market for corn and oatmeal.

A little beyond Gearstones, where the road bears left, a track carries straight on, striking up the hillside opposite onto **Cam Fell**. There is no mistaking this as the Roman road, which ran from near Ingleton to Bainbridge, in Wensleydale. It was long used in later times, being adopted by the Lancaster and Richmond turnpike. However in 1795 the old route over Cam Fell was superseded by an easier line, the road about to be followed, crossing into Widdale and reaching Wensleydale at Hawes.

Although only marked on the definitive map as a footpath, its history would suggest that the proper classification of the Cam Fell Road should be as a bridleway, so affording cyclists an official right of way. Not that anyone is likely to object to its use by cyclists, or even that you are likely to meet anybody. In any case the scope for riding as opposed to pushing is slight. In a mile it is joined by the old packhorse road from Horton, via Birkwith, described in Route 17 together with its continuation over Cam Fell.

Beyond the junction of the old and present roads the latter resumes its upward course, gradually at first, through bleak surroundings. In the middle of nowhere a branch leads across into Dentdale (Route 16) and a little further, at **Newby Head**, is the road summit (437m). The farm just before it was another one-time inn, which like that at Gearstones survived into this century. The first house on the Widdale side was also licensed for a time — travel must have been slow in those days! The long descent through Widdale calls for little comment. It is a good fast road, apart from a short hill about 2 miles before **Hawes**. For Hawes and Wensleydale see Route 22.

ROUTE 21
KIRKBY LONSDALE to SEDBERGH and DENT

Distances from Kirkby Lonsdale (miles): **Devil's Bridge** $^1/_2$, **Caster-ton** $1^1/_2$ (Dent $9^1/_2$), **Barbon** $3^1/_2$, **Middleton** 6, **Sedbergh** (via A683) 11, **Rash Bridge** $10^1/_2$ (Dent 14).

INTRODUCTION

The scenery in the vicinity of Kirkby Lonsdale has long been praised — longer, in fact, than the Dales, with their barer, wilder beauty. The Lune valley is excellent cycling territory from its source almost to the sea, and its broad vale between Kirkby Lonsdale and Sedbergh offers some of the best and easiest riding.

There are a number of roads between the two towns. First and foremost is the A683, which is very quiet since the M6 took away what little long-distance traffic it carried. Parallel to this is a narrow almost-forgotten lane running through Barbon.

On the west side of the river there are various lanes running north from Kirkby Lonsdale itself: almost devoid of traffic and offering excellent views across to the western flanks of the Dales. One of these is followed by the Cumbria Cycleway before this crosses the Lune to the main road.

Two roads from Kirkby Lonsdale to Dent are included: the direct road, following the pretty side-valley of Barbondale, and that along the south side of the Dee, opposite Sedbergh. If coming from the direction of Ingleton these and the main road up Lunesdale can be joined near Casterton, cutting out the Kirkby Lonsdale corner, but it is a bit churlish to miss such an interesting old place for the sake of a few miles. The town is described in Route 18.

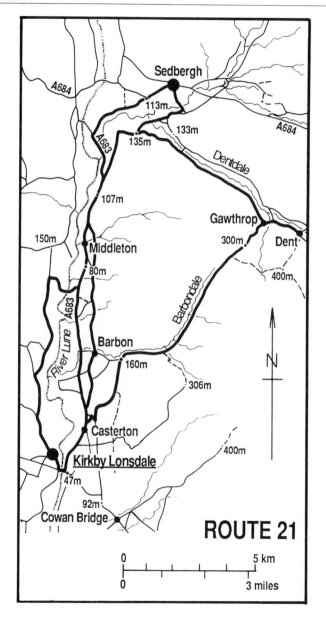

ROUTE 21

THE ROUTE

If Kirkby Lonsdale has been approached via the Devil's Bridge, rather than return that way continue through the town, turning right out of the B6254 in a mile (signposted Mansergh). This is a delightful back-road up the west side of Lunesdale by which slow but stately progress may be made all the way to Sedbergh. Alternatively, after passing the imposing ruin of Rigmaden, a right turn doubles back to cross the Lune and join the main road 6 miles below Sedbergh.

From **Kirkby Lonsdale** town centre join the A65, immediately turning left for the road down to **Devil's Bridge**. Just across it is the Sedbergh road. The river scenery hereabouts is most charming and both old and new bridges are imposing structures.

The A683 is an excellent cycling road. It keeps to the valley bottom with only the easiest of hills all the way to Sedbergh and it is merely a case of ticking off the milestones. Only the diversions from it require any comment. The one village on the main road is **Casterton**, a pretty spot, just beyond which the direct road to Dent branches off.

The Casterton to Dent route (8 miles) cuts up to the old Roman road, running due north, which is followed only briefly before the road turns right, to slant round the foot of the hillside at an easy angle, with excellent views across the Lune. Soon the narrow Barbondale is entered, the road accompanying the tumbling stream as it gradually attains an altitude of 300m. The descent into Dentdale is very steep. For Dent and Dentdale see Route 16.

The main road passes west of the village of **Barbon**, which is worth including whether bound for Sedbergh or Dent. From it a narrow lane continues northwards, barely a stone's throw from the A683 yet so hemmed in with tall hedges, that it seems to be in a world of its own. The surface is somewhat neglected in parts. This lane rejoins the main road just beyond the hamlet of Middleton and near Middleton Hall.

Beyond Middleton the main road rises to cross under the old railway. Three-quarters of a mile further, where it dips again to cross the Rawthay, a narrow unsignposted road carries straight on. This jinks about and threatens to give up completely in one or two places but continues, rather overgrown and bumpy, round the northern tip of Holme Fell with marvellous views across to Sedbergh and the Howgill Fells. At a fork one branch, little more than a cart track, drops to Millthrop and Sedbergh, the other carries round into Dentdale, dropping to the riverside at **Rash Bridge**. Here you are as well crossing to the regular road, which has a better surface and easier gradients than the road forward via Gawthrop. For **Sedbergh** and **Dent** see Route 16.

ROUTE 22

WENSLEYDALE: LEYBURN to HAWES (CIRCULAR)

Distances from Leyburn (miles): **Wensley** $1^1/_2$, **West Witton** $3^3/_4$, **Aysgarth Falls** $7^3/_4$, **Aysgarth village** $8^1/_2$, **Worton** $11^3/_4$ (Askrigg 13), **Bainbridge** $13^1/_4$, **Hawes** $17^1/_2$.
Return distances from Hawes: **Hardraw** $2^1/_4$, **Askrigg** $7^1/_2$, **Carperby** 12, **Castle Bolton** $14^1/_2$ (Richmond 29), **Wensley** $18^1/_2$, **Leyburn** 20.

INTRODUCTION

Second only to Wharfedale in size and interest, Wensleydale has much to offer the cyclist. Perhaps nowhere else in the Dales is the character of the area better exemplified than in travelling west from Leyburn, where the hills really start to hem in the river, to Hawes. Here the geological structure of the Dales is well illustrated, with its prominent topography of level-topped hills, limestone scarps and shale screes. These combine to give the landscape a sweeping, brooding quality that is unmistakeably Wensleydale.

The valley is well populated and prosperous and the only major one which is traversed by an 'A' road. However this carries negligible end-to-end traffic (despite efforts to get it defined as a primary route) and the small amount of local traffic need not deter the cyclist.

The scenic attractions of Wensleydale are both natural and man-made — stone-walled fields, old towns and villages, Semer Water, tucked away in its own side valley, and a great number of waterfalls. Of these Aysgarth Falls, on the Ure, and Hardraw Force, on a tributary, are the best examples, but there are many others which, while less spectacular, provide a pleasant digression from pursuit of the open road. Overall though, it will be the longer and expansive views of the dale which will leave the greatest impression.

The main points of interest, working up the valley from Leyburn, are Wensley Church, Bolton Castle, Aysgarth Falls, the old town of Askrigg, picturesque Bainbridge and Semer Water, Hawes (the main centre for the upper dale) and nearby Hardraw Force. To include all of these in a single trip up the valley calls for some careful planning. However there are two roads between Wensley and Hawes which lend themselves to a round trip and for convenience this will be how the valley is described — outward along the A684 and returning by the unclassified road along the north side. The various crossings into Swaledale are also included in their appropriate place. Out of all this each cyclist should be able to pick a route to suit him or herself.

THE ROUTE

If coming from the south **Leyburn** can, of course, be bypassed by the direct road from Middleham Bridge to Wensley, which cuts out the hill up to the town. Leyburn contains no castle, ancient church or historic buildings to trouble the guidebook writer yet, as an example of a small market town serving its rural hinterland in an unassuming way, it is hard to find an equal, unless it be Hawes. Once nearby Wensley was the market town for this end of the dale, but the devastation created by a visit of the plague in the sixteenth century caused a migration up the hill. Later road improvements helped to put Leyburn 'on the map'. Sojourners at Leyburn should take a stroll along the Shawl, as a grassy terrace stretching for some way west of the town is known. It introduces one to the stepped formation of Wensleydale, which is revealed far below. The walk begins at the far corner of Commercial Square.

Some distances from Leyburn (miles): **Reeth** 8 (Route 31), **Richmond** $11^1/_2$ (Route 29), **Bedale** $10^1/_2$, **Northallerton** (nearest railhead) $18^1/_2$, **Masham** 11 (Route 29), **Kettlewell** $17^1/_2$ (via Coverdale, Route 30).

Between Leyburn and Bedale there are various alternatives to the main road, but follow a map, not signposts. Perhaps the most interesting way is round via Jervaulx Abbey (14 miles, see Route 29).

Heading up the dale from Leyburn, there is a long descent to **Wensley**, a small village but once a town of sufficient importance to give its name to the whole valley (the alternative name Yoredale reflects an earlier spelling of Ure). The church has many features of historic interest.

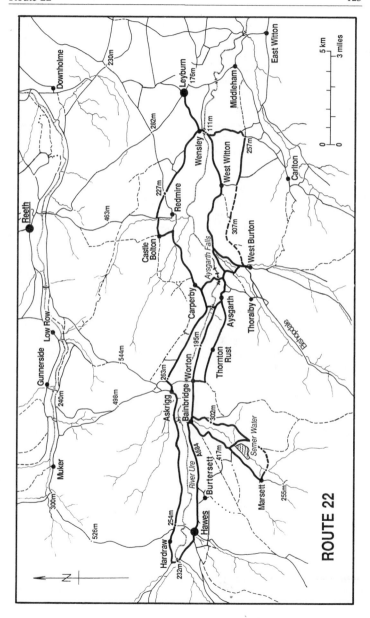

ROUTE 22

Wensley to West Burton via Middleham High Moor is an interesting diversion for those with time and energy to spare. From Wensley Bridge take the Carlton road to its highest point (257m), where turn right. This road soon runs along the edge of an escarpment which provides an excellent view across the dale. At the next junction take the road down to the right a little way, keeping straight on where this doubles back to West Witton. Note the old eighteenth-century guidestone on the corner. This directs one along an ancient green road, with a good metalled surface, though little of the main valley can now be seen. Before commencing the descent to West Burton climb to the crags on the left — Morpeth Scar — for a panoramic view over Wensleydale, Bishopdale and Walden.

Beyond Wensley Bridge the road regains all the height lost from Leyburn as it rises to West Witton. On the climb there is a good view of Bolton Hall, built 300 years ago to supersede Bolton Castle as a residence. The castle, glimpsed beyond, will be passed on the return journey.

West Witton is a straggling village which once housed workers at the lead mines on Penhow Hill. The road continues high on the valley side before dropping to cross the foot of Bishopdale. **West Burton** (Route 4) one of the most picturesque villages in the area, lies about a mile to the south and can easily be included en route. There is a good view up Bishopdale on the steep ascent to **Aysgarth**. For the falls turn right before the top, by the Youth Hostel. This road drops very steeply to an old mill (now a carriage museum) and the fine arched bridge which spans one of the prettiest sections of the Ure.

Aysgarth Falls are actually a series of three cascades which are spread along a mile of the river. The Upper Falls are just above the bridge and form a most attractive view from it, the limestone slabs bordering the bed of the river providing a popular bathing place. The Middle and Lower Falls can be reached from the road along the north bank, just where it turns sharp uphill. Here cycles must be left. A path runs through the woods some way above the river, eventually cutting down to it near the Lower Falls. It is possible then to work upriver to the Middle Falls, but there is no easy way back up to the main path. A little higher along the road are the information centre, toilets and a cafe. The return road to Leyburn (9 miles) via Castle Bolton is described later.

Returning to the main road more uphill follows to Aysgarth village, which boasts an old cross but is otherwise unremarkable. At the far end of the one street there is a choice of route forward: the A684, dropping to the river again, or a lane through the pretty village of **Thornton Rust**.

Gayle and Hawes in Upper Wensleydale

This latter road follows one of the special features of Wensleydale, a limestone terrace high along the valley side and remarkably consistent in level. There is a similar length of road across the valley between Askrigg and Carperby. Views across the valley are excellent. The main road is rejoined at Worton, where the river may be crossed for those wishing to include both Askrigg and Bainbridge on the way up-dale (there is also a footbridge just west of Aysgarth which links the two roads). Keeping to the main road there is a steep drop into Bainbridge where the River Bain, one of the shortest in England, is crossed below some stepped falls.

Bainbridge is a well built village surrounding a spacious green, on which are situated the old stocks. It is a place of great antiquity as it was situated at the foot of the Roman road which ran over Wether Fell, and the hill just east of the village was the site of the Roman fort of *Virosidum*. Bainbridge is still orientated north-south with the main road jinking through it. In Norman times the village stood at the boundary of the Forest of Wensley, which included all the upper valley of the Ure and which was reserved as a hunting chase. During the winter months a horn was sounded each night to guide travellers in this wild region and the custom is still kept up, the horn being kept at the Rose and Crown Inn. The inn itself dates back to 1445. On the Bain is Low Mill, a fully-restored corn mill open to the public on certain days.

Semer Water

Bainbridge is the obvious starting point for a visit to Semer Water, one of the few natural lakes in Yorkshire, situated about 3 miles to the south. Its location cannot be presupposed from the village, as this side valley is extremely narrow: as a result although the lake is only about 50m higher than Bainbridge the cyclist has to toil up twice this climb to get to it. There are two roads, similarly profiled, one for going and one for coming back. Each involves a steep climb out of Wensleydale followed by a level section and ending with a steep drop to the lake foot, on which care is required.

Opinions on the picturesqueness of the lake and its surroundings vary considerably: probably the weather holds the key to this, as on an overcast day it can appear an extremely bleak sheet of water. On sunnier occasions it presents a much more attractive picture, a deep bowl enclosing blue water and rich green fields which contrast with the barer fellsides. Formerly the lake was about twice its present size, but 50 years ago was lowered to release land for agriculture. Few motorists penetrate to the head of its valley — Raydale — but the roads to Stalling Busk and Marsett are linked by a track (prone to flooding in wet weather) which provides the cyclist with a rewarding if hilly circuit of the lake. This upper part of the valley is very sheltered and verdant. The suffix -sett in many of the local place names is from the old Norse *setr,* a seat or homestead. It is more commonly corrupted into -side, as in Gunnerside.

From Semer Water one can cross into Wharfedale via the old road over Stake Moss, most of which is rideable. There is also a bridleway from Countersett which eventually meets the Roman road up from Bainbridge. Both these tracks are fully covered in Route 5. Most visitors will return to Bainbridge, but those who tackle the precipitous direct road to Hawes will be rewarded with excellent views over the lake and Wensleydale.

The main road from Bainbridge to Hawes calls for little comment, a general uphill trend but no hills by Dale's standards. **Hawes** is one of those little towns whose importance is out of proportion to its population — about 1,100. It is a bustling market town and undisputed 'capital' of Upper Wensleydale, with no rival within 15 miles. It is a very hospitable place, with numerous inns and cafes, a Youth Hostel and a National Park Information Centre at the old railway station. Next door to this is the Upper Dales Folk Museum. At the Hawes Ropemaker one can watch ropes being made.

The name of the town is derived from the Anglo-Saxon *haus* a hill pass, and seen from the Buttertubs road to Swaledale its focal position at the foot of a number of radiating valleys will be appreciated. Yet the town is not that old: it only developed about 200 years ago when it began to overtake Askrigg in importance. In 1795 the new road from Ribblehead through Widdale was made and the future of Hawes was assured. There is nothing special in the town, yet it is a satisfying place to wander round — a town surviving on its ability to serve the customer whether dalesman or tourist.

Some distances from Hawes (miles): **Buckden** 12, **Grassington** $22^1/_4$ (Route 5), **Settle** 22 (Routes 16 and 23), **Ingleton** $16^1/_2$ (Route 20), **Dent** $13^1/_2$ (Route 23), **Garsden Station** $6^1/_2$, **Sedbergh** $15^3/_4$ (Route 23), **Kirkby Stephen** $16^3/_4$ (Route 24).

The route from Hawes to Swaledale, via the Buttertubs Pass ,begins with the road which crosses the Ure and then the minor road along the north of the valley, after which it climbs very steeply, easing off through the hamlet of Simonside. It then steepens again, to 1 in 6. Above a cattle grid the open moor is reached and the gradients less severe, but there is still a mile or so to the summit (526m). A sharp descent brings one to the Buttertubs themselves, deep hollows in the limestone. Beyond them the road contours high above a deep side valley before a splendid descent into Swaledale. The dale is described in Route 26. Hawes to Thwaite is $6^3/_4$ miles, Muker $7^1/_2$ miles.

Hawes to Askrigg

The return down Wensleydale via the north side of the valley is most easily reached by the Buttertubs road, from the east end of the town. By this road it is $5^1/_2$ miles to Askrigg from Hawes. However the immediate objective is **Hardraw Force**, which is most profitably reached by continuing west from Hawes to Appersett, there crossing the Ure and returning down valley. The way to the fall (small entrance fee) lies through the Green Dragon pub and up a little gorge. The fall 'the highest single-drop fall in England' is nearly 30m. It is formed by resilient limestone overlying weaker rock, which has worn away enabling one to walk behind the curtain of water.

The road along the north side of the valley through Hardraw was the original 1760s turnpike road from Sedbergh to Askrigg, so missing out Hawes. One or two of the old cylindrical milestones survive. Keeping as this road does some way above the valley floor there are good views across Wensleydale. A mile short of Askrigg one may cross the valley to Bainbridge.

Askrigg is an ancient place and once the main market town in Wensleydale. It had a number of rural industries and was also famous for clock-making. By the end of the eighteenth century it had begun to decline, one reason being the expansion of Hawes. The curving main street is lined with old three-storey buildings and in front of the church are the market cross and the old bull-baiting ring.

> While not as spectacular a fall as Hardraw Force, the walk up the leafy Mill Gill to Mill Gill Force provides a pleasant contrast to the wild, sweeping scenery of this part of Wensleydale. Take the lane which runs alongside Askrigg Church. At a gate ($^1/_4$ mile) cycles must be left: here the path cuts across a field on the right, bridges the stream and follows the rim of a pretty dell before descending to the foot of the waterfall.

Askrigg to Swaledale

Askrigg is the focus of a number of hill crossings to Swaledale, as befits its former importance. These are among the longest and steepest ascents in the Dales.

> For Upper Swaledale (Muker $5^3/_4$ miles, Gunnerside 6 miles) the climb on the Wensleydale side is unbroken and a pure slog, though the rearward views, which include Semer Water, are good. The Swaledale side is more interesting, with a choice of road either side of Oxnop Gill. That on the eastern side is not signposted at either end, but leaves the other road just past the summit (498m). It is shown 'uncoloured' on most maps but despite its upper sections being rather grass-grown it is perfectly rideable with reasonable care. Owing to its poorer surface and the number of gates, it is perhaps less suitable northbound than southbound. With a very steep descent it meets the main road along Swaledale at Satron, a mile west of Gunnerside.
>
> The direct Muker road drops steeply from the summit, running below Oxnop Scar and then drops in fits and starts. The final descent to the B6270 is extremely steep and fully merits its 1 in 4 rating, unlike many better-known hills in the Dales. This is the route of the Yorkshire Dales Cycleway between Wensleydale and Swaledale.
>
> For Lower Swaledale (Reeth $8^3/_4$ miles) it is an even longer ascent from Askrigg, to an altitude of 544m. Beyond the moorland summit — The Fleak — the road drops into a wild moorland hollow, then bears east to run along a terrace high above a deep side valley, with excellent views over Swaledale. After the long descent to the riverside it is best to cross the Swale to the B6270, as the direct Grinton road involves more hillclimbing.
>
> Half a mile beyond the Fleak, where the Reeth road turns right, a good track drops to Summer Lodge, the terminus of a tarred road up from Crackpot. Travelling from Swaledale this provides a reasonable alternative to the road, but coming north the relatively rough state of the drop to Summer Lodge is poor reward for effort put in on the Wensleydale side.

Askrigg

Askrigg to Leyburn

From Askrigg the Leyburn road dips, then climbs steeply to gain a limestone terrace, which dips very gently downhill as it is followed east. Below it is Nappa Hall, in part dating from the fifteenth century. Beyond Woodhall the road drops to near the Ure and a side turning leads to a footbridge across the river and the main road to Aysgarth village. The turning to Aysgarth Falls (see above) comes just before Carperby, a neat village with another fine old cross.

On the falling gradients beyond Carperby there are good views of Bolton Castle, which in some ways looks more impressive from the valley below than from close up. Although the hill to it might seem off-putting the forward road, through Redmire, eventually rises to the same height so the climb to the castle will not be wasted. **Redmire** is another pleasant village, despite the nearby quarries. It has a part Norman church tucked away down a side turning.

Bolton Castle dates from the time of Richard III and had an active early history, including the detention here of Mary Queen of Scots. It was subjected to siege in the Civil War and afterwards rendered indefensible. The owners later moved to Bolton Hall. Part of the castle is now a restaurant while the remainder is open to the public. A major restoration programme has been completed. The adjacent village is known as Castle Bolton, to distinguish it from the castle itself.

Redmire or Castle Bolton to Reeth is 6 miles and a hilly crossing of no particular interest. Turning off in Redmire, the road rises to cross the direct Castle Bolton-Leyburn route. There is a long and steady climb past quarries, until the road levels out above Apedale. This bare valley, once given over to leadmining, is traversed by a good track, which in clear weather may easily be continued into Swaledale. The road resumes its climb to the moortop followed by a mile or so of level before the corresponding long descent to Grinton. The Youth Hostel is a little way up the Leyburn road.

From Castle Bolton the road to Leyburn heads east through the village, reaching in a mile or so the road from Redmire to Reeth. At first there appears to be no road forward. However a gate almost opposite leads onto a narrow lane which contours along the hillside giving excellent views across Wensleydale to Penhill and back to Bolton Castle. In $^3/_4$ mile it meets a second road from Redmire, near to where this forks to Richmond and to Leyburn. Coming west the short cut is not signposted, but should certainly not be missed. It forms part of the Yorkshire Dales Cycleway.

The Richmond branch — the old turnpike from Askrigg — rises to 310m at **Scarth Nick**, a well known viewpoint, but is otherwise a dull road. The best route to Leyburn is to keep down the valley to Wensley, mainly on falling gradients, then back up the main A684 for the last mile or so.

ROUTE 23
HAWES to SEDBERGH (CIRCULAR)

Distances from Hawes (miles): **Moor Cock Inn** 5$^1/_2$, **Garsdale** 9$^1/_2$, **Sedbergh** 15$^3/_4$.
Return distances from Sedbergh: **Dent** 5$^1/_2$, **Cowgill** 9$^1/_4$, **Newby Head** (junction) 12$^1/_2$, **Hawes** 19.

INTRODUCTION

Most of Wensleydale's links are with the larger towns to the east — Harrogate, Northallerton, Darlington etc — so this western exit from the dale is comparatively free of traffic. Nor is there any mighty pass to be surmounted, the watershed between Wensleydale and Garsdale being only about 80m higher than Hawes. This is thus a good cycling road and one which forms a convenient link between the Dales and the Lake District, proceeding by the considerably less friendly road from Sedbergh to Kendal. By returning through Dentdale a scenically very interesting circular trip can be had from Hawes.

THE ROUTE

The early stages of the road from **Hawes** are delightful, the road falling to the river at Appersett. Note the railway viaduct spanning the dell to the left: although disused, popular pressure saved it from demolition. The Ure is crossed by the 'New' Bridge, for beyond the old turnpike from Askrigg, the original main road up the valley, is joined. There is a climb to and beyond the turning to Cotterdale, a small side valley with no special attraction to the cyclist, then a drop to Thwaite Bridge. Thereafter, a long but gradual ascent brings one to the highest point of the crossing, just before the Moorcock Inn. Beyond the inn the road rises to pass under the railway viaduct, more or less on the watershed between Wensleydale and Garsdale. Cumbria is now entered.

Garsdale Head is a bleak spot and consists of little more than a row of cottages near the station and a few scattered farms. Like Ribblehead it was the site of a shanty town during the construction of the railway and indeed the railway was long the focus of its existence. The station was the junction of the branch to Hawes. The road up to the station continues over the hill to Dentdale and is described in Route 16.

The road into Garsdale is excellent — all downhill for the next 4 miles, keeping company with the River Clough. The hilly old road, soon looping off to the right, gives access to Grisedale, a sheltered upland valley. It is of no particular interest, and most definitely a dead end for the cyclist. Presently signs introduce one to the 'village' of **Garsdale**, generally known as The Street, and lying in the widest and greenest part of the valley. Beyond, the road winds about a great deal, with another loop of the old road (gated and hilly) branching off to the right.

Nearing Sedbergh the road runs across Longstone Fell, the valley opening out to reveal a splendid view of the town backed by the sprawling Howgill Fells. This viewpoint is the start of a very interesting short walk, the Sedgewick Geological Trail, which runs along the River Clough below.

The trail commemorates Adam Sedgewick of Dent, whose study of the area provided the first insights into modern geology. The trail proper starts at Danny Bridge on the minor road coming down the valley. Below it the river tumbles over inclined beds of limestone to where these abruptly give way to older uplifted rocks. This is the Dent Fault — geologically where Dales and Lakeland meet. The descriptive leaflet is necessary to explain it fully, though anyone would find it a delightful walk.

There follows a long drop to the Rawthey Bridge followed by a short uphill to the town. The main street (no entry) lies off to the right. For **Sedbergh** see Route 16.

The Sedbergh to Kendal road (11 miles) at the turn of the last century was described in the *Cycling Touring Club Road Book* as 'one of the worst main roads in England. It abounds in steep hills, is almost wholly of loose or stony surface, and the greatest care must be exercised throughout'. The surface is now satisfactory, but the hills are still there. There are good views throughout, however. The main climb begins beyond Lincoln's Inn Bridge, across the Lune, about $2^1/_2$ miles from Sedbergh, the road rising 180m. The summit is about half a mile beyond the motorway bridge. The road onwards is by no means straightforward, the main descent not coming until the outskirts of Kendal are reached.

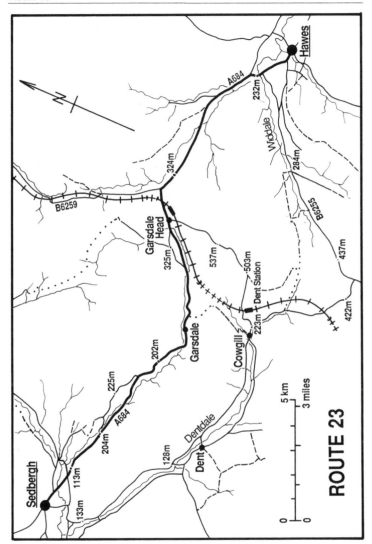

Sedbergh to Hawes via Dentdale and Widdale
As far as Newby Head this is more fully described the reverse way in
Route 16. From **Sedbergh** the road drops to bridge the Rawthey, with

a climb then past Millthrop as it enters the narrow valley mouth of Dentdale. The remaining four or so miles to **Dent** town provide easy cycling; indeed the road is one of the best cycling roads in the Dales. For Dent see Route 16. Beyond Dent the road on the north side of the valley is preferable, as that across the river is a little hillier. The valley rises only gradually to **Cowgill**. Here the road up to Dent station provides an alternative way back to Hawes, described in Route 16. The route by Newby Head is much to be preferred — it shows you the full length of Dentdale, there is 100m less climbing to face and the descents are more suited to fast riding.

Beyond Cowgill, **Dentdale** continues to provide some delightful riverside stretches and it is not until Dentdale Youth Hostel is passed that the gradient steepens for the long rise out of the valley. After passing under the railway viaduct it is about a mile to the hilltop, a little beyond which is the junction with the Ingleton-Hawes road (Route 20). Turning north there is a slight climb to the one-time inn at Newby Head.

Beyond the summit (437m) there is a splendid descent through Widdale, with scarcely a pedal turned in anger in the 4 miles to Snaizholme Bridge. Here a tributary valley is crossed. **Widdale** is rather ordinary: small groups of trees shelter the few farms, with more recent plantations breaking up the otherwise bare hillsides. The road has a nice section above the river, after which it swings away to cross an intervening ridge before descending into Wensleydale. Those who explore the little lane down to Appersett will find this a more pleasant way to **Hawes.** For the town see Route 22.

ROUTE 24
KIRKBY STEPHEN to HAWES

Distances from Kirkby Stephen (miles): **Nateby** $1^1/_2$, **Pendragon Castle** $4^1/_4$, **Outhgill** 5, **Moor Cock Inn** $11^1/_4$ (Dent $20^1/_2$), **Hawes** $16^3/_4$.

INTRODUCTION

This is a splendid route through wild mountain scenery. First climbing the upper valley of the Eden — Mallerstang — it crosses to the headwaters of the Ure, but the impression is of one continuous valley, bordered by steep-sided hills. For cycling the road is reasonably good, with no long ascents and rather a number of short hills. The railway summit (the highest point on the Settle and Carlisle line) is alongside that of the road and so gives an idea of the hillclimbing to come.

As might be expected, this link between two such major river valleys has been a line of communication for thousands of years. Within 5 miles of Kirkby Stephen it passes three defensive strongholds — Wharton Hall, Lammerside Castle and Pendragon Castle — which gave some protection from raids by the Scots. In later, more peaceful times, it became a busy drovers' route, with various lines of road still traceable. The present road dates in part from the 1820s, after which it monopolised traffic. One earlier route which can be followed by the rough-stuff cyclist is the famous High Way, running along the eastern shoulder of Mallerstang into Wensleydale.

THE ROUTE

As well as the road via Nateby, as described below, there is a bridleway route west of the river as far as Pendragon Castle. This starts as a good minor road to and beyond Wharton Hall, a fifteenth-century peel tower, with additions from the sixteenth century and later. Half a mile beyond the hall a track (bridleway) bridges the river to the B6259. The road forward, which is

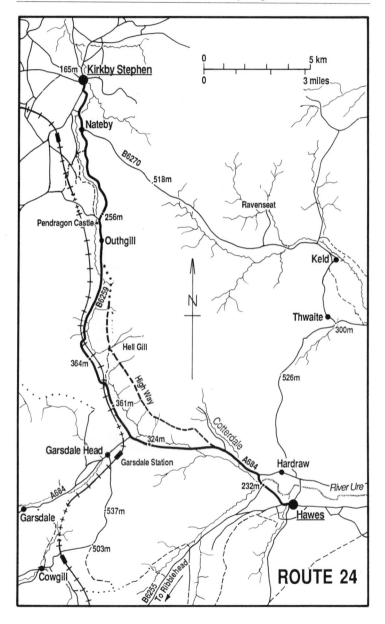

0   5 km
0   3 miles

165m **Kirkby Stephen**

Nateby

B6270

518m

Ravenseat

256m

Pendragon Castle

Outhgill

Keld

N

Thwaite

300m

B6259

Hell Gill

526m

364m

High Way

361m

324m

Cotterdale

Garsdale Head

Garsdale Station

A684

Hardraw

A684

River Ure

232m

Hawes

Garsdale

537m

503m

Cowgill

B6255
To Ribblehead

ROUTE 24

private, continues up to Low House and the public road then to the A683. The official bridleway (unmarked) makes its way across fields direct to Lammerside Castle. This is a small and rather unsafe looking ruin, unimpressive from the outside. Just beyond is the foot of the public road, which continues as a riverside cart track to Pendragon.

For **Kirkby Stephen** see Route 25. From the town there is a steady rise to **Nateby**, where the Keld road can be seen winding across the lonely fells to Swaledale. Beyond Nateby the road levels out, the prelude to a few easy miles through ever-enclosing hills. Across the valley is a glimpse of Lammerside Castle. After a short riverside section the road reaches **Pendragon Castle**. Although no more extensive than Lammerside, the legend that it was originally built by Uther Pendragon, father of King Arthur, has given it a cloak of romance. The present remains are of a twelfth-century structure, probably a typical peel tower. Whatever its full history, it is most gloriously placed, backed by Wild Boar Fell. From the castle a side road climbs out of the valley to the Sedbergh road and Ravenstonedale.

Outhgill is the only hamlet in Mallerstang and even so is just the tiniest of places. From here onwards the road gradually steepens as it climbs up to the watershed.

The High Way commences at a gate about half a mile south of Outhgill. Allow a minimum of $2\frac{1}{2}$ hours from road end to road end (about 8 miles). The start is most inauspicious,and discouraging, a boggy cart track slanting up the hillside. The first mile is hard work until, on reaching the limestone, it is transformed into a firm green road, providing excellent going. The valley bottom has now disappeared, and to ride alone among the surrounding mountains is an unforgettable experience. The road descends over a limestone plateau to Hell Gill Bridge, which spans the infant River Eden. The river tumbles unseen in the depths of the narrow ravine, so steep-sided as to defy exploration. It can only be safely glimpsed from the bridge.

South of Hell Gill Bridge the broad green track onwards leads down, in a mile or so, to Shaw Paddock on the main road. The High Way aims for High Hall, atop the line of trees on the horizon. The path is indistinct at first but later obvious. In a short distance it fords the headstream of the River Ure.

Nearing High Hall the path is joined by a wall which perseveres until the A684 is reached. The general trend remains slightly uphill, resulting in little cycling in this direction. First a barn and then a ruined farmhouse, High Dyke, are passed. The latter was formerly the High Way Inn. The railway viaduct at Garsdale Head is conspicuous, though appearing tiny, while hills rise in all directions.

Shortly after High Dyke the track gains the lip of a limestone plateau

High Hall

and the going becomes much easier, nearly all rideable. At its highest point, 500m up, it emerges overlooking Wensleydale. The track winds down to a wicket gate , then a steep but firm grassy track leads straight down alongside the wall. This section is just about rideable, with good brakes and nerves. At the foot of this steep section bear left to enter the A684 by a gate. It is 3 miles on to Hawes.

After crossing the River Eden the road climbs up to the boundary between Cumbria and North Yorkshire. This is the highest point reached by the road (364m), but so up and down are the next 5 miles that there is no chance to ease up. In a headwind it can be hard going. At Shaw Paddock, where the road dips under the railway, a good track leads up to **Hell Gill Bridge** (see above). About $^3/_4$ mile further a track on the left leads through a plantation down to the old chapel of **Lunds**. This small sombre building stands alone in a rough field near the infant Ure. It is devoid of the slightest concession to appearance and with its group of ancient gravestones seems to epitomise the struggles of past generations in this wild and unforgiving country.

Pursuing the B6259, the **Moorcock Inn** is soon reached, a welcome sight for the traveller. It was built following the turnpiking of the Kirkby Stephen road in the 1820s. A mile west is Garsdale railway station.

Moorcock Inn to Ribblehead (for Ingleton, Settle etc) is $12^1/_4$ miles via Dentdale (see also Route 16). Total ascent is 455m. This is the more interesting way, but very hilly. From Garsdale Head it is a climb up past the station along the Coal Road, then a long and steep descent to Lea Yeat in Dentdale. There is a pleasant run for a few miles up-valley, then long steep hill up to the Hawes road at Newby Head.

Moorcock to Ribblehead is $14^3/_4$ miles via Appersett (see also Route 23). Total ascent is 290m. Follow A684 as described below, then cut up side lane at Appersett to join B6255 from Hawes. It is a long but mainly gradual climb through Widdale to Newby Head, then a good downhill run to Ribblehead.

To take a train from Garsdale Station is by far the easiest option, but remember that there are not that many trains. Northbound trains do not stop at Ribblehead.

The Moorcock Inn is only about 50m higher than Hawes, and although running down the ever-widening valley of the Ure the road is far from the steady descent one might hope for. In fact all the way to Leyburn, or even Masham, the main road is characterised by a tendency to shy away from the valley bottom if it can. As far as this section is concerned, the only noteworthy hill lies beyond Thwaite Bridge. Hardraw, with its famous waterfall, is only just off-route. For **Hardraw**, **Hawes** and the whole of Wensleydale see Route 22.

ROUTE 25

AROUND THE HOWGILL FELLS: SEDBERGH to TEBAY and KIRKBY STEPHEN

Distances from Sedbergh (miles): **Howgill** $2^1/_2$, **Low Borrow Bridge** $7^1/_2$, **Tebay** $9^1/_2$, **Ravenstonedale** $16^3/_4$, **Kirkby Stephen** $21^1/_2$, **Cautley Beck** (inn) 31, **Sedbergh** $35^1/_2$. **Kendal to Tebay** $11^1/_2$.

INTRODUCTION

The Howgill Fells rise majestically to the north of Sedbergh and provide a magnificent, yet little known, walking area. The cyclist is limited to the peripheral roads, but these are quiet, scenic and in their own way as pleasant. The route described is a circular one, providing a tour of 28 miles, or 36 miles if Kirkby Stephen is included, as it should be. Tebay is the starting point for a number of good cycling routes extending north into the Eden Valley and some brief notes on these are included.

The first part of this route runs through the Lune Gorge, which also carries the main west coast railway line and the M6. One can wonder how many cyclists, travelling by faster modes of transport, have looked across the valley to the little minor road running along its eastern side and resolved to one day seek it out and ride along it. Today's the day!

THE ROUTE

The road turns out of **Sedbergh's** main street near the church (sign-posted Howgill) and rises steeply, giving a good view down the Vale of Lune. At the next junction (note the old guide post) it picks up the line of a Roman road, running north, and continues as a narrow tall-hedged lane to the hamlet of **Howgill**. Entering the Lune Gorge the road ascends

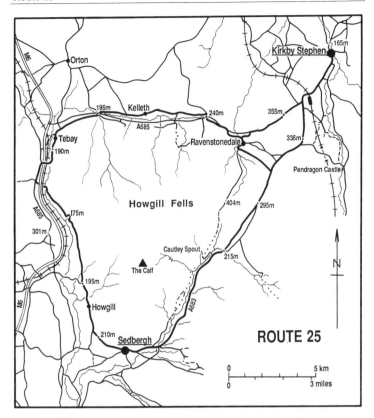

ROUTE 25

to work its way along the flank of the fell, while across the valley the railway and motorway squeeze along the hillside. Where the road descends to cross a beck an old wayside stone, now defaced, marks the one-time boundary between the West Riding of Yorkshire and Westmorland, the latter administered from Appleby, the former from Wakefield 80 miles away! Eventually the road crosses the Lune and winds up to meet the A685 from Kendal at Low Borrow Bridge. From here some more undulating cycling brings one to Tebay, where the valley broadens out considerably.

When steam ruled on the main line over Shap summit **Tebay** was an important railway centre, for nearly all trains would require a banking engine. It was also the junction for the lonely line over Stainmore to Darlington, which brought Cleveland ore to the ironworks at Barrow.

Tebay has a distinct 'railway village' south of the older settlement, but now it is the motorway rather than the railway which brings employment. There is a Youth Hostel in the village — easy access from the M6 boasts the YHA handbook!

Despite the importance of the Lune-Eden watershed in communications, the area north of Tebay is one of the least visited in northern England. Yet this is excellent cycling territory, with a number of useful routes leading towards the Lake District or linking up with the Cumbria Cycleway to Carlisle.

From Tebay there is an undulating climb to Orton, a well built village formerly of more importance: here the Shap and Appleby roads separate, rising to 325m and 344m respectively. From Shap one can proceed to Haweswater ($6^1/_2$ miles) or Penrith, but for the latter a more pleasant way is down the Lyvennet Valley through Crosby Ravensworth and then via Morland and Cliburn. This way it is 21 miles from Tebay to Penrith. The Appleby road provides distant views of the Pennines towering over the Vale of Eden: especially conspicuous ahead is the deep rift of High Cup. Although mainly downhill there are one or two short climbs before Appleby. Tebay to Orton is $2^3/_4$ miles, Shap $9^1/_2$ miles and Appleby $12^3/_4$ miles.

Between Tebay and Kirkby Stephen the road, A685, is almost all of new construction, as far as Newbiggin on the course of the former railway. This keeps to the valley bottom, but the tourist will seek out the old road, via **Kelleth**, along the northern slopes of the valley and offering the better views. Although slower than the new road it will be found the more pleasant and is almost devoid of traffic (not that the A685 is ever busy).

There is a gradual ascent to Newbiggin, after which the old road loops off again and should be followed to the village of **Ravenstonedale**. This is one of the prettiest spots around, way off the usual tourist beat and too far away from any large town to be 'commuterised'. Its situation in an oasis of greenery on a tributary of the River Eden should be savoured, as from here to Kirkby Stephen is a dull moorland crossing. Ravenstonedale Church has a number of old features and a pair of cottages retain their old wooden galleries: these were once very commonplace in the hand-knitting villages, as well as in such towns as Sedbergh and Dent.

From the village two roads run east, one providing the shortest way back to Sedbergh (11 miles) and the other, after crossing the A683, descends to Pendragon Castle ($4^1/_2$ miles, Route 24). There is also an old drovers' road running south from Ravenstonedale direct to the Rawthey Valley. As far as Adamthwaite this is now tarred, while the remainder of the way is a scenic green track, but muddy.

Lune Gorge

At Ravenstonedale a decision must be made on whether to cut up to the main Sedbergh road, so returning direct, or continuing over Ash Fell to Kirkby Stephen. It has to be admitted that this latter road has nothing in itself to recommend it: there is a rise of 110m one way and 160m returning from Kirkby Stephen to the summit on the Sedbergh road. The diversion adds nearly 8 miles to the itinerary. Still, **Kirkby Stephen** is one of those old-fashioned northern towns which few would want to miss. While there are no particular 'sights' its main street has a number of handsome buildings, the overall effect very pleasing. Adjacent to the Nateby road is Skenkrith Park, on the Eden, where the river tumbles down a limestone gorge.

Some distances from Kirkby Stephen (miles): **Appleby** 11, **Alston** 36, **Penrith** 24, **Brough** $4^1/_4$, **Middleton-in-Teesdale** $18^1/_2$ (Route 32), **Barnard Castle** 22 (Route 32), **Tan Hill** $11^1/_4$ (Route 28), **Reeth** 23 (Route 26), **Hawes** $16^1/_2$ (Route 24).

The railway station, on the Settle to Carlisle line, is a good $1^1/_2$ miles from the town and all uphill.

From Kirkby Stephen to Sedbergh, rather than retrace your route for a few miles, venture up Mallerstang via Wharton or Nateby to Pendragon Castle (see Route 24). This substitutes valley byways for moorland highways.

The various roads from Kirkby Stephen, Pendragon and Raven-stonedale meet on the moors, with wild lonely hills extending in all directions. To the south-east rises Wild Boar Fell. The Sedbergh road rises a little way to the watershed (295m), from where it is downhill to the outskirts of that town. This road is an excellent one, probably the quietest 'A' road in England, with gradual gradients and the scenery improving in richness with each mile. The Cross Keys Inn (unusual in being owned by the National Trust, and having no licence) is the usual starting point for the walk to **Cautley Spout**, a cascade high on the stream coming down the valley on the right.

The falls are just visible from the road, but the walk up to them, while not revealing any new attractions, is a popular one. The Rawthey is bridged just north of the inn and the path soon strikes up the side valley. Its lowest sections are apt to be muddy. The Howgills are seen at their most dramatic — these are real mountains, unlike the smooth hills of the Dales.

The remainder of the run to **Sedbergh** is an easy one down the Rawthey Valley, and beautiful throughout. The only uphill is the final pull up to the centre of the town. For Sedbergh see Route 16.

ROUTE 26

SWALEDALE: RICHMOND to KELD and KIRKBY STEPHEN

Distances from Richmond (miles): **Grinton** 10, **Reeth** 11, **Feetham** 14^1/$_2$, **Gunnerside** 17, **Muker** 20 (Hawes 27^1/$_2$), **Thwaite** 21^1/$_4$, **Keld** 23^1/$_2$ (Tan Hill 27^3/$_4$), **Hollow Mill Cross** (summit) 29^1/$_2$, **Kirkby Stephen** 34.

INTRODUCTION

Each of the major dales has its own character and perhaps none is more individual than the narrow and winding Swaledale. The impression of depth is emphasised by the lack of a level valley bottom as found in Wensleydale or Wharfedale, and the surrounding hills, though no higher than elsewhere, are more steeply sided. Characteristic of the upper dale are the grey stone villages and the numerous barns, seemingly one in every field, which dot the lower hill slopes.

Swaledale is now wholly agricultural, but this was not always the case. The higher ground, mainly to the north but also extending into Wensleydale, was rich in lead ore, which was worked as early as the Roman occupation. The industry was most active in the eighteenth and nineteenth centuries, when it became the main source of employment in the valley, particularly in Arkengarthdale, north of Reeth. There was a rapid decline at the end of that century, followed by much emigration from the area. Remains of once-thriving communities linger on amidst the remains of the industry, which nature is gradually obliterating. Scenically the impact is now slight and does not impair the beauty of Swaledale. The valley is still largely uninfluenced by tourism and though it is acquiring the usual trappings of potteries, craft and tea shops these can be tolerated as bringing new life into old communities.

The best cycling in the dale is the main A6108/B6270 route between

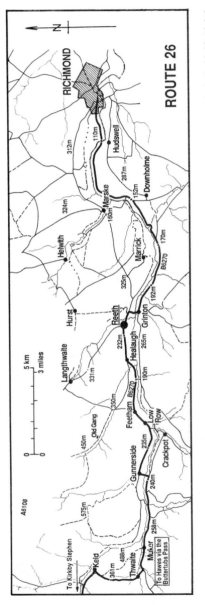

Richmond and Thwaite. Through traffic to Kirkby Stephen is almost non-existent and the relative remoteness of the valley means that it does not suffer the influx of day and weekend visitors to the extent found elsewhere. This valley road can hold its own with any in the Dales and is an excellent one for cyclists with no long hills, and the short ones can be excused for taking one from the banks of the Swale, to some lovely viewpoints. Apart from this main route the side roads will be found hard going, as are the moorland roads leading out of the valley. Indeed, the only easy way in or out of Swaledale is via Richmond and no finer day excursion is there than from that town, working slowly up the dale, exploring its byways and communities, then returning down the B6270, a straightforward run of a few hours at most. Keld, about 24 miles from Richmond, is probably the best place to turn round, as nearby is some pretty river scenery, while the roads beyond are relatively dull. But first a few words about Richmond itself.

The town of **Richmond** grew up around the castle, a Norman stronghold built shortly after the Conquest. It provided an ideal location, with the cliff falling away on three sides to the Swale, far below, while on the north side the massive keep completed the defences. This keep still stands to its full height and from the top there is an excellent view over the busy market place of the town.

Richmond has borne the passing of the centuries lightly. Civil strife and industrial expansion have largely passed it by, and there is a timelessness about many of its steep cobbled streets and narrow ginnels. It is a compact town which requires exploration on foot. After visiting the castle and walking around the outside of the walls drop down to The Green and Richmond Bridge, which now carries only the minor road to Hudswell. From the riverside there is a good view of the castle. Return via Cravengate and Newbiggin. In the market place itself is Holy Trinity Church: no longer a place of worship, it houses the Regimental Museum of the Green Howards. Leaving the market place by King Street on the left is the Georgian Theatre, a unique eighteenth-century survival, excellently restored to its original condition. There is a theatre museum. The nearby Greyfriars Tower is all that remains of a never-completed church.

Some distances from Richmond (miles): **Barnard Castle** 15^1/$_4$ (Route 33), **Bishop Auckland** 22, **Darlington** 13, **Yarm** 23 (Stockton 27), **Northallerton** 15^1/$_2$, **Masham** 15, **Leyburn** 11^1/$_2$ (Route 29), **Castle Bolton** 14^1/$_2$ (Route 29).

A short distance from Richmond are the remains of Easby Abbey. The abbey occupies a confined site by the Swale and together with the adjacent church of St Agatha forms a most picturesque scene. It can be reached by following the Catterick road, or by footpath along the riverbank (a mile from the A6136 bridge).

THE ROUTE

The present main road from **Richmond** to Reeth is comparatively modern, superseding the hill roads through Marske to Reeth (Route 27) or over Hudswell Moor to Leyburn and Wensleydale. This accounts for the lack of any intermediate settlements in the 10 miles to Grinton, in contrast to the succession of villages higher up. It is noticeable that in several places this road suffers from subsidence, so perhaps those earlier road builders knew what thay were doing in spurning the valley bottom.

From Richmond the road drops to and crosses the Swale, then runs through a pleasant gorge topped with limestone crags. Five miles from the town the Leyburn road branches off and the Reeth road continues up the valley. In a mile or so look out on the right for the scanty remains of Ellerton Priory (Cistercian), of which little but a narrow tower survives. A little further on, and across the river, is Marrick Priory

(Route 27).

Grinton is a venerable place, once the only place of importance in Swaledale and much older than Reeth, now visible across the valley. Grinton Church has some interesting features. Grinton Lodge Youth Hostel is half a mile south of the village on the hilly direct road to Leyburn. A minor road continues along the southern side of the valley, but this is rather hilly and the visitor will probably wish to see Reeth first.

Reeth was the capital of the old leadmining area and remains the nearest thing to a town that the dale possesses. It suffered severely from the collapse of its main industry but now, like the rest of Swaledale, extends a welcoming face to the visitor. There are plenty of pubs and tea shops and a small but good folk museum, all gathered round the spacious, if hilly, village green. For the road up Arkengarthdale to Tan Hill etc see Route 27, for the road to Barnard Castle Route 31.

There is a resemblance of a hill out of Reeth — probably the only one worth mentioning between Richmond and Thwaite — then the road descends gradually to the riverside beyond **Healaugh**.

Healaugh is the best starting point for a visit to the most extensive remnants of the leadmining industry, the Old Gang Smelt Mills. A side road runs up to meet the Feetham-Langthwaite road, near the junction with which are the ruins of the Surrender Smelt Mill. A mile higher up this side valley, and reached by following a good track (bridleway) are the Old Gang Mills, 380m up.

Here were several dressing floors, where the ore was crushed and waste material separated, and a smelting mill, where the ore was reduced to the pure metal. The furnace required a strong blast of air, which was created by a long flue running up the hillside (a common and very noticeable feature of the old leadmining areas). This would terminate at a chimney, where a strong fire would supply a draught. Just above Old Gang a line of stone pillars marks the old peat store, 120m long, where fuel would be kept. At the smelt mills another chimney served the blacksmith's forge. Ore was brought to Old Gang from a wide area, much of it passing underground through inter-linked tunnels.

The bridge beyond Healaugh provides a useful link to the roads and tracks along the south side of the Swale. The fell road across to Askrigg — arguably the toughest in the Dales — is described the reverse way in Route 22. A few hundred yards across the Swale Bridge a delightful green lane turns out of the Askrigg road and runs above woods reaching down to the river. It is one of the loveliest byways in Swaledale. At Low Houses it becomes a tarred road, after which another bridge enables the

Crackpot Hall

B6270 to be regained.

On the north side of the river the road runs through **Feetham** and **Low Row**, which together form a single straggling village embracing other old communities that cling to the hillside. From Feetham a very hilly road strikes north to Langthwaite ($3^3/_4$ miles) in Arkengarthdale. The gradients are such that cyclists are as well going round via Reeth, unless visiting the Old Gang Smelt Mills.

A little beyond Low Row a side road out of the B6270 crosses the river to **Crackpot**. The name is said to mean Crow-Hole, a reference to a cave nearby.

Crackpot lies high above the Swale at the mouth of a deep side valley, but there is nothing in the hamlet itself to compensate for the 1 in 6 climb — not even a sign to be photographed beside. The road continues on much easier gradients to Summer Lodge, whereafter a good but steep track continues the climb up to the Askrigg road (Route 22). From Crackpot one can also continue up Swaledale by a minor road which runs high above the valley floor with fine views, meeting the B6270 beyond Gunnerside. There is also a riverside bridleway between the two Swale bridges, but this is usually wet and muddy.

Gunnerside is most easily reached by keeping to the main road, which squeezes in between the river and the steep wooded hillside. It is a nicely-situated village, at the foot of Gunnerside Gill. This has some fine scenery and can be readily explored on foot. There is also a pleasant field path to **Ivelet** (a mile each way), where there is an ancient bridge spanning the Swale with a magnificent high single arch. This is crossed by a minor road from Gunnerside, a hilly alternative to the B6270.

> Gunnerside to Keld via the Swale Gorge is a beautiful route, and one offering the best of off-the-road cycling. Allow at least an hour to Keld.
>
> Take the minor road west from Gunnerside which climbs steadily before a nasty dip to cross the Ivelet Beck. On the far side the tarred road continues as far as Ramps Holme Farm, just north of Muker. Here a good cart track (bridleway) continues forward to the side of the Swale, which it follows through the deep gorge of the river all the way to Keld. The track is rideable throughout. After crossing Swinner Beck it rises up the valley side, giving good views back to Muker. Near the hilltop a track doubles back to the ruins of Crackpot Hall, undermined by old lead workings, and a sad sight in such beautiful surroundings. The main track continues along the hillside, high above the unseen Kisdon Force.
>
> Opposite Keld a branch path leads down beside the fine East Gill falls to a footbridge, a very pretty spot (see below), where a narrow muddy path turns up to the hamlet. The better route is to keep to the north of the Swale, joining the Tan Hill road in $^3/_4$ mile, then returning to Keld.

Beyond Gunnerside the main road crosses the Swale and continues on the south side of the valley. At Satron an unsignposted road crosses to Askrigg, in Wensleydale, though the regular route (and Yorkshire Dales Cycleway) turns off a mile further (see Route 22). A little beyond Satron a road to the right drops to Ivelet Bridge, mentioned above, and some pretty riverside scenery. Continuing along the B6270 a pleasant run brings one to **Muker**, a delightfully-situated village in growing popularity as a tourist centre. It is the last place of any size in Swaledale. Until its church was built all burials had to take place at Grinton, the route taken down the valley becoming known as the Corpse Way.

At Muker the main road and the River Swale part company to go their separate ways around Kisdon Hill, being reunited at Keld. The river gorge above Muker contains some of the finest scenery in Swaledale and some excellent walks can be had, whether for a mile or so or all the way to Keld and back. The Swale Gorge can, of course, be cycled through by means of the bridleway from Gunnerside, as described above, but there is only a footpath link from Muker to Ramps Holme Bridge. One bridleway route from Muker, easily followed but involving 240m of ascent, is the old Corpse Way over Kisdon Hill to Keld.

Thwaite

Muker to Hawes by the Buttertubs Pass (7¹/₂ miles)

This turns out of the B6270 a mile west of Muker and just above the hamlet of Thwaite. The road is wider than most inter-valley routes and even carries a bus service on summer weekends. From the road junction there is a steady climb for a mile or so and on reaching a double bend the gradient increases, but nowhere near the 1 in 4 threatened on the signposts. Over one's shoulder is Kisdon Hill, almost the same height as the first summit to be reached, about 210m above Thwaite.

From this point the road offers a good view back down Swaledale and into the deep valley of the Cliff Beck, one of the steepest-sided in the Dales. Descending a little the road reaches the **Buttertubs**, deep cavities worn in the limestone alongside the road. Despite giving their name to the pass they are not especially impressive, but provide a good excuse for a break before the final climb to the watershed. This is really steep, but it is only a short way to the moorland summit, 526m. The road onward barely drops at all for nearly a mile, then commences a long but problem-free descent into Wensleydale. Beyond its tributary valley of Widdale is seen the flat top of Ingleborough, while due south the road up to Fleet Moss may be discerned. At the T-junction at the hill foot turn right if visiting Hardraw Force before Hawes.

Muker to Keld and Kirkby Stephen

A short run brings one to **Thwaite**, where the village store is the last shop in the valley. Thwaite also marks the end of the 20 odd miles of easy cycling from Richmond: from here on the going is much harder. The road to Keld rises 80m to Angram, with good views back down the valley.

Keld stands high above the Swale which here is reunited with the road. The village lies mostly down a side turning, from the foot of which a path leads to its main tourist attraction, the waterfalls. Keld Youth Hostel stands on the main B6270. There is a lot of fine scenery in the vicinity of Keld, and given the many miles of bleak moorland between here and Kirkby Stephen it is as well to take some time to explore the locality.

Many visitors to Keld walk down to the riverside, snap the waterfalls on East Gill under the impression that these are Kisdon Force, and then return to their cars. This is perhaps as well, as the true Kisdon Force is a good 15 minutes' walk from the hamlet and difficult to find, let alone get to. The route follows the Pennine Way south, then the branch path to Muker. A little way down this a path turning through a gap in a wall doubles back to the falls, which are set in a deep limestone gorge. The final approach is precariously muddy. There is no proper path along the river back to the footbridge — one would be an advantage — so return the way you came.

Nearer Keld the East Gill Falls are very pretty and provide some nice picnicking spots. The path to them over the Swale Bridge is a bridleway, though cycles will need to be wheeled. Across the river it meets the lane along the north and east side of the gorge from West Stonesdale down to Ivelet and Gunnerside, described above.

Beyond Keld the B6270 gradually drops to the Swale near the head of its long limestone-topped gorge. There are a whole series of waterfalls as the river runs over its rocky bed. Note also the old lime kilns. At Park Bridge a side road heads north to Tan Hill.

Keld to Tan Hill ($4^1/_4$ miles) is thirsty work. After crossing the Swale this immediately starts a twisting 1 in 4 ascent, before the gradient eases through the cluster of farms comprising West Stonesdale. The valley beyond is exceptionally bleak. Any hikers passed will be drop-outs from the parallel Pennine Way — there is always someone worse off than you! Another very steep climb to the old coalmines in Mould Gill brings one to the relatively easy last stretch, though the inn is a long time appearing.

The Kirkby Stephen road continues by the riverside for about a mile, then crosses to the north bank and begins a steep climb up the moor. The

Swaledale, near Keld

turning for Ravenseat marks the top of the hill, as the road onwards, although still notionally ascending Birkdale, bobs around the 450m contour for the next 3 miles. The scenery is desolate. The road then steepens again for the final push to the watershed between the Swale and the Eden. This is Hollow Mill Cross and though the cross is no more there are two boundary stones, 100m apart, a consequence of past territorial disputes between adjoining communities. The view westward is an extensive one, comprising Mallerstang, the Howgill Fells, the distant hills of Lakeland and the green low-lying Vale of Eden, into which the road now plunges. The gradient is 1 in 5 in places, but on the whole the descent is care-free, provided close watch is kept on the wandering sheep. The total descent to Kirkby Stephen is 350m, considerably more than such famous passes as Fleet Moss or the Buttertubs. At Nateby note the old AA sign on the pub wall. There is another fastidious signpost on entering **Kirkby Stephen**, a short run further. For the town see Route 25.

ROUTE 27
RICHMOND to REETH VIA MARSKE

Distances from Richmond (miles): **Marske** 5 (Marrick 8),
Reeth $9^1/_2$. **Marrick to Reeth** $2^3/_4$.

INTRODUCTION

Until about 1840, when the present A6108 up the valley floor was constructed, the routes from Richmond to Upper Swaledale were the old packhorse roads, keeping to the moors. On the south side of the valley one led through Hudswell and Downholme to Grinton; on the north side ran the road to be described, through Marske.

As a cycling route its gradients tell against it, there being a total of 420m of ascent between Richmond and Reeth, compared to 110m by the main road. Its only merits are its historical interest and lack of traffic: scenically the riverside route is superior and certainly advisable if there is the slightest headwind.

The area north of Marske is a remote one, rarely visited: rolling moorland with deep incised valleys. It is now thinly populated and in large measure given over to military training, but up to a hundred or so years ago bustled with the lead mining industry. A look at a large scale map will reveal many traces of the industry and the network of tracks and roads, many now long-forgotten, to serve it. Some notes on these routes are included, but the area is well off the tourist beat and the lone cyclist should keep to well defined tracks. In addition some areas are closed to the public during firing practice, others at all times.

THE ROUTE

For **Richmond** see Route 26. Taking the A6108 west from the town centre, the old road turns right, as Hurgill Road, rising steadily for the next 2 miles. Despite its elevation the views, moorland in character, are uninteresting and the deep Swale Gorge, only a little to the south, is

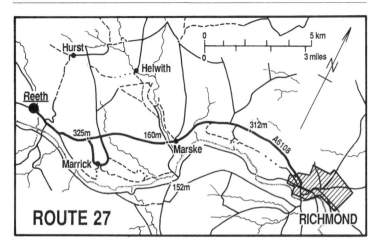

ROUTE 27

hardly to be guessed at.

About 3 miles from Richmond a side road descends very steeply to Apple-garth. A footpath from this junction, keeping to the wall on the left reaches, in 5 minutes, the top of Whitcliffe Scar, a limestone cliff overlooking the Swale and an excellent viewpoint.

Continuing along the road there is a long descent into the greener scenery of Clapgate Gill, then a run across a plateau to **Marske**, the only intermediate place between Richmond and Fremington, near Reeth. It is nicely placed on the hillside above Marske Beck.

The deep valley of the Marske Beck, running north from the village, is one of the sweetest, an appearance emphasised by its dour moorland surroundings. It may be followed by a bridleway from the village through Clints to Orgate House, there crossing to meet the road up the opposite side, which is tarred to that point and can be used to return to the Reeth road. If continuing north, for Newsham and Barnard Castle, one can take an old track, still in good condition, which turns out of the road up the Marske Beck just north of Skelton. This climbs high above the valley before dropping to Helwith. On the way Richmond Castle can be seen down the Swale Gorge. From Helwith a tarred road runs north to Holgate crossroads, where the route from Reeth via Hurst (Route 31) is joined. This crossroads can also be reached by the hilly and dull road from Marske (5 miles). Another 5 miles of moorland road brings one to Newsham, for Barnard Castle (see Route 33).

From the bridge at Marske a turning leads down to the main Richmond-Reeth road at **Downholme Bridge** and, although longer, is the easiest route to either place. Marske to Leyburn is 8 miles.

Beyond Marske the direct Reeth road climbs once again, a long 1 in 6, bringing one up onto the rolling moor. A ruined building in the valley to the left is an old smelting mill. After a dip the road from Marrick to Hurst is crossed. **Marrick**, although a mile or so off-route, is perhaps worth the slight detour involved. Perched high above Swaledale, it is well spread out, unlike the huddled villages of the valley bottom.

Cyclists can easily reach Marrick Priory, next to the riverside, by turning from the direct Reeth road, at the foot of the hill. An alternative way, practicable with a bicycle but not easy to find, is by the narrowest of lanes (bridleway) heading south from the village. It forms the continuation of the lane leading past the priory. There is also a pleasant walk leading down from the village by the 'Nuns' Steps'.

Marrick Priory was built in the twelfth century as a house for Benedictine nuns. It is now used as a diocesan youth centre. There is no bridge across the river hereabouts.

Returning to the Reeth road, this is met at its highest point (325m). In a little way a fine view of Swaledale is revealed on the steep descent to the valley bottom. At the foot of the hill is the road back to Marrick Priory, then it is an easy mile or so to Reeth.

For Reeth and Upper Swaledale see Route 26, for Reeth via Arkengarthdale to Tan Hill and Brough see Route 28.

ROUTE 28
REETH to TAN HILL and BROUGH

Distances from Reeth (miles): **Langthwaite** $3^1/_4$, **Tan Hill** $11^1/_2$, **Barras** $16^3/_4$, **Kirkby Stephen** $22^3/_4$, **Brough** 21. **Richmond to Reeth** is 11 miles either via the main road (easy, Route 26), or the much hillier road via Marske (Route 27).

INTRODUCTION

This road, following the valley of the Arkle Beck-Arkengarthdale, is predominately a moorland one. Only in the vicinity of Langthwaite is there any of the pretty riverside scenery so commonplace elsewhere in the Dales, while it needs a really clear day to reveal the fine panorama down the Eden Valley from Barras.

The roads out of Arkengarthdale are very ancient and were long busy carrying the produce of the lead mines, coal extracted from the pits on Tan Hill, and cattle being driven south. Now they lie off the main arteries of communication and apart from the inquisitive tourist, little traffic disturbs the loneliness of the moors.

The lead mining industry of Arkengarthdale probably goes back to Roman times but the great expansion took place in the eighteenth century. It reached a peak in the late nineteenth century, but thereafter suffered a rapid decline. The principal mine-owners were the Bathurst family, whose initials are preserved in the 'CB' Hotel at Langthwaite and on old boundary stones still to be seen alongside the road in the vicinity of Tan Hill. Until the lead industry developed the valley was thinly populated: during its expansion small communities sprung up adjacent to the mines — often just a row of cottages on the hillside — yet perpetuating the old Norse names of earlier settlers. Arkle Town, Booze and Whaw are three examples which will intrigue the visitor.

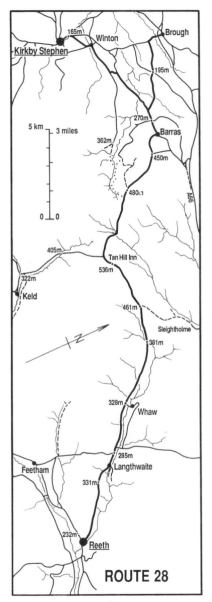

Kirkby Stephen
165m — Winton — Brough
195m
270m
5 km — 3 miles
Barras
362m
450m
480m
A66
405m
Tan Hill Inn
536m
322m
Keld
461m
N
Sleightholme
381m
328m
Whaw
285m
Feetham — Langthwaite
331m
232m — Reeth

ROUTE 28

THE ROUTE

The road from **Reeth** up Arkengarthdale spurns the valley floor and strikes up the eastern flank of Calver Hill. The steep escarpment opposite — Fremington Edge — is pock-marked with old mineral workings. Overall the road rises steadily for about 2 miles from Reeth, to where the moor drops away to reveal a fine picture of the sheltered dale, with its scattered farms and houses set around a finely placed church.

Langthwaite is the largest settlement in Arkengarthdale, yet the tiniest of villages. From the main road a bridge leads across the Arkle Beck into a little square, with an inn, a shop, and tightly huddled cottages.

> If you can cycle up the precipitous hill to Booze you deserve a drink — but you will not get one! A better plan is to make a circular walk of it (about 2 miles). Booze is a scattered hamlet of now just a few cottages and farms, with several buildings derelict and crumbling. Keep bearing right along the road. At Town Farm turn right onto a footpath (no signpost) which leads down through meadows, heading for Storthwaite Hall. Before this is reached turn right onto a cart track which drops through woods to the riverside for the return to Langthwaite.

Beyond Langthwaite the road once again climbs away from the

Tan Hill Inn

steep valley bottom, passing the church and 'CB' Inn. Just past the junction with the Barnard Castle road, from which it is better seen, is the old hexagonal powder house, where gunpowder for the mines was stored. The Tan Hill road keeps to the south side of the dale, which after a mile or so broadens into a bleak moorland basin. Although the general trend is up, the ascent is broken by frequent dips to cross tributary valleys, the principal one being **Punchard Gill**. On the hill beyond is the old Punchard Gate House, site of the former toll gate. Eventually the Arkle Beck itself is crossed, after which the gradient steepens as the road rises to cross the watershed. On the climb a side-road joins, coming up from Bowes (tarred as far as the last farm, Sleightholme, then metalled but all easily rideable). Bowes to Tan Hill is $8^3/_4$ miles.

From the hilltop the view north is revealed. It is totally featureless, unless one counts the movement of traffic on the distant A66. The road continues much as before across the moorland for a few more weary miles, eventually reaching its summit level of 536m just before the Tan Hill Inn.

The **Tan Hill Inn** has survived, when so many less remote inns have closed, from its distinction in being the highest in England. It has the further advantage in being on one of the least hospitable sections of the Pennine Way. It provides a warm welcome to the passing visitor, though in winter it can often be snowed up for weeks on end. The inn once catered for cattle drovers and miners at the surrounding coal workings, which were worked commercially until the 1930s.

Tan Hill to Keld is ($4^1/_4$ miles). Extreme caution is required about $^3/_4$ mile south of the inn, where the combination of a bend, steepening gradient and loose surface creates a dangerous corner. Otherwise the road provides a good descent down West Stonesdale save for a slight rise after crossing the beck. The final drop to the Swale is at 1 in 4, on which a branch track on the left leads along the north side of the river, eventually reaching Gunnerside. For Keld and vicinity see Route 26. By continuing down the B6270 for 2 miles (long downhill after an initial rise from Keld) one reaches the foot of the Buttertubs Pass to Hawes (Route 26).

The way on from Tan Hill to Brough or Kirkby Stephen continues as the bleakest of moorland roads. In about 2 miles it crosses the watershed between the tributaries of the Tees and the Eden, and gradually a deep valley, that of the River Belah, opens up on the left. Across it, on the skyline, may be discerned the **Nine Standards**, one of the least accessible of Britain's stone circles. The road maintains a consistent height of about 450m for some way before commencing one of the longest hills in the Dales. On the way, the old railway over Stainmore is crossed at the site of the onetime Barras Station. This served the few neighbouring farms: there is no village of Barras as such. From hereabouts there is a grand panorama over the Vale of Eden, on a clear day stretching to the Scottish borders. On the right is the long escarpment of the Pennines, culminating in their highest point, Cross Fell; to the west are the Lakeland mountains, though not seen at their best.

After a long straight hill the Brough and Kirkby Stephen roads separate. The former branch drops to cross the Argill Beck, then pursues an undulating course, with Brough Castle prominent ahead. For **Brough** see Route 32. Although a 'dead end' as regards the A66, those travelling on to Appleby ($9^1/_2$ miles) can continue through the village and then proceed through Great Musgrave and Warcop, which avoids most of the main road.

The Kirkby Stephen branch falls steeply to cross the River Belah, with a good view upstream of its winding gorge. Thereafter the road is more level to Kaber and its junction with the A685 2 miles short of Kirkby Stephen. A very narrow side lane (signposted Rookby) cuts the corner slightly, through **Winton**, a village especially rich in interesting old houses. For a description of **Kirkby Stephen** see Route 25.

ROUTE 29
RICHMOND to LEYBURN, MASHAM and RIPON

Distances from Richmond (miles): **Downholme** $5^3/_4$, **Halfpenny House** 8 (Castle Bolton $14^1/_2$) **Bellerby** $9^3/_4$, **Leyburn** $11^1/_2$, **Middleham** $13^3/_4$, **East Witton** $15^1/_2$, **Jervaulx Abbey** $17^1/_4$ (Ellingstring $19^1/_2$), **Masham** $22^1/_2$ (15 direct), **West Tanfield** $26^1/_4$, **Ripon** 32.

INTRODUCTION

This route skirts the Dales, without penetrating them. It takes the only easy crossing from Swaledale to Wensleydale and south of Leyburn runs past a number of places of interest, in particular Middleham Castle and Jervaulx Abbey. Although an 'A' road throughout it is not busy and on the whole provides good cycling, the gradients becoming ever easier as you progress south.

There are a number of unclassified roads south from Richmond to Leyburn, Masham etc which look tempting on the map but which have the disadvantage of crossing much higher ground. In practice these will be found to offer little if any time savings; also Catterick Garrison generates a lot of traffic in the area. If seeking an alternative route south the author's recommendation would be via Brompton, Catterick and Hackforth to Bedale (12 miles), a pleasant little town, then either to Masham ($6^1/_2$ miles) or direct to Ripon (12 miles). This traverses easy cycling terrain throughout, but not Dales' Country.

THE ROUTE

For **Richmond** see Route 26. The Leyburn road runs up the beautiful Swale Gorge for 5 miles before turning south. A gradual climb past Downholme and Walburn Hall (part sixteenth century) leads to

East Witton

Halfpenny House, where the old hill road from Richmond to Redmire is joined, to be followed for nearly a mile.

> The road forward to Redmire and Castle Bolton continues to rise over uninteresting moor to Scarth Nick, where an excellent view of Wensleydale is revealed. For Castle Bolton bear right again (no signpost) immediately on joining the road from Leyburn at the foot of the hill (see Route 22).

From the A6108 turning it is nearly all downhill through **Bellerby**, to **Leyburn**. For the town and the roads up Wensleydale see Route 22.

Beyond Leyburn the cyclist should note that the next two villages, Middleham and East Witton, stand on top of hills, with the road dropping to the level of the Ure before, between and after them. Middleham Bridge, with its imposing castellated towers, was an early suspension bridge of 1828, but later rebuilt into its present form.

A glance round the old market place at **Middleham** will confirm that this was once a place of some importance. It is still well supplied with cafes and inns for the traveller's needs. A little further up the hill and towering over the houses is the castle, quite interesting, although comparatively little known for its size. In the thirteenth century it became the property of the Neville family, who constructed what was in effect a second castle around the original Norman keep. During the Wars of the Roses it came into the possession of Richard III until his

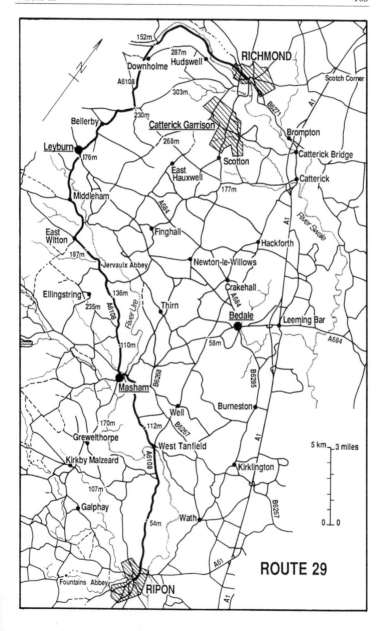

death at Bosworth Field. Later its destruction was ordered by Cromwell, but it continued in use as a residence for some time. The castle is overlooked by a much earlier hill fort, from which fine views are obtained.

Middleham is a famous centre for racehorse training and these can often be seen being exercised on Middleham Moor, which rises from the west end of the village.

A digression into the side valley of Coverdale provides a change from the A6108. It is more fully described in Route 30. Two miles from Middleham are the scant remains of Coverham Abbey, and by crossing the old bridge nearby the main road can be regained at East Witton. To get a better impression of the dale one can travel as far as Carlton (mainly uphill), returning via West Scrafton to East Witton. This adds about 10 miles to the main road distance.

Beyond Middleham the A6108 falls to cross the River Cover just above its confluence with the Ure. Spanning the latter is Ulshaw Bridge, an ancient and picturesque structure. On it is a sundial dated 1674. Although now just carrying a minor road the bridge was once a major crossing on the road from Kendal to York.

The next village, **East Witton**, comes as a surprise, two rows of stone cottages facing each other across a linear village green. The place was rebuilt from scratch by the owner of the estate, the Marquis of Ailesbury, at the beginning of the nineteenth century. In earlier times it had been a market town. A couple of miles further the road passes the entrance to **Jervaulx Abbey**, which is a few minutes' walk from the road.

This Cistercian abbey was re-established here in 1156 from an earlier site near Askrigg. The name is correctly pronounced 'Jarvis', and simply means 'Ure Vale'. Most of the surviving work dates from the twelfth and early thirteenth centuries. The ruins are extensive and not easy to interpret without a ground plan, but may be enjoyed purely as a maze of linked walled lawns, set in fine parkland. While the site may not possess the majesty of Fountains it does provide an interlude of relaxation for the wayfarer before you resume the journey.

Two miles south of Jervaulx and high above the valley is the village of Ellingstring, where there is a Youth Hostel. East of Jervaulx a minor road crosses the Ure at Kilgram by another fine old bridge. This road may be continued via Thirn and Thornton Watlass to Bedale which is $8^1/_4$ miles from the abbey. It is very pleasant cycling.

Jervaulx Abbey

After skirting Jervaulx Park the A6108 rises a little to run below a wood. It is then more or less level to **Masham**, for the centre of which you will need to turn out of the main road. See Route 13.

Masham to Kirkby Malzeard, etc is described the reverse way in Route 13. As well as running to Fountains Abbey it provides a hillier alternative to the main road for Ripon, by turning off at Grewelthorpe or, preferably, Kirkby Malzeard. Distances from Masham are Kirkby Malzeard $4^3/_4$ miles, Ripon 11, Fountains Abbey 10 and Pateley Bridge $13^1/_4$.

From Masham the River Ure is crossed, then the A6108 commences a long but gradual climb with good views back over the town to the high country beyond. After Binsoe a steep hill sweeps down to **West Tanfield**. Here the main point of interest is the Marmion Tower, adjoining the church. It is a remnant of the fortified house of the Marmion family and dates from the fifteenth century. It is occasionally open to visitors. The church contains monuments of the Marmions. The view from the Ure Bridge of the tower and church is a fine one.

From West Tanfield there are some pleasant lanes east of the Ure by which Ripon can be reached in about 8 miles. The direct A6108 is virtually level throughout and unremarkable. Mid-way is the entrance to Lightwater Valley, a leisure park and a popular family attraction. For **Ripon** see Route 11.

ROUTE 30
COVERDALE: LEYBURN
to KETTLEWELL

Distances from Leyburn (miles): **Middleham** $2^1/_4$, **Carlton** 7 ($5^1/_4$ via Wensley), **Horsehouse** $9^1/_2$, **Kettlewell** $17^1/_2$, **Grassington** $23^3/_4$.

INTRODUCTION

This road is minor but an ancient one. Ogilby's *Brittania* (1675), one of the first practical guides for the traveller, incorporates it as part of the route from the West Riding to Richmond and Newcastle. The top sections were only surfaced for motor vehicles in 1952 and it was one of the last roads in the Dales to retain gates, the final one being replaced by a cattle grid in 1984. As a through route it is scenically inferior to that via Bishopdale and Buckden to Wharfedale (about 3 miles longer from Leyburn) and overall a fair bit hillier, including a 300m drop into, or rise out of, Kettlewell. Comparisons apart, however, it will be found a rewarding road.

THE ROUTE

From **Leyburn** there is a choice of going via Wensley or Middleham. The latter way is the more interesting and easier, though a mile or so longer.

The Yorkshire Dales Cycleway takes the shorter route via Wensley. From the turning beyond Wensley Bridge there is a stiff ascent, with good views first over Wensleydale and then Coverdale. At the road summit a lane to the right runs high above the valley, offering excellent views. Coming from Upper Wensleydale to Coverdale, this is perhaps a better way to join this route than the tougher direct road over the hill to Melmerby. From the hilltop it is an easy onward run to where the road via Middleham is met, a little short of Carlton. Wensley to Carlton is $3^3/_4$ miles.

Middleham, with its once-mighty castle, is well worthy of inspection, and is described in Route 29. From Middleham the onward road is a pleasant run, mainly ascending, to Coverham Church, where a side turning leads to the site of Coverham Abbey. Little remains of this premonastratensian building, save for a few arches and other stonework. The fine steeply-arched bridge should also be admired. Across it runs a lane which leaves the main Masham road at East Witton, and a very pleasant run it is too, but this unfortunately misses out Middleham if coming from the Masham direction. A mention must also be made of the very quiet road up the southern side of Coverdale from Coverham Bridge to **West Scrafton**, a pretty little village. This is a little hillier than the usual road through Carlton.

From Coverham Bridge the going is more upward to and through **Carlton**. This is the largest settlement in the valley: even so the houses either side of the long village street back straight onto the fields. One of the cottages on the right bears an inscription commemorating Henry Constantine, the 'Bard of Coverdale'.

Beyond Carlton the scenery is not as good, with less greenery and variation, though

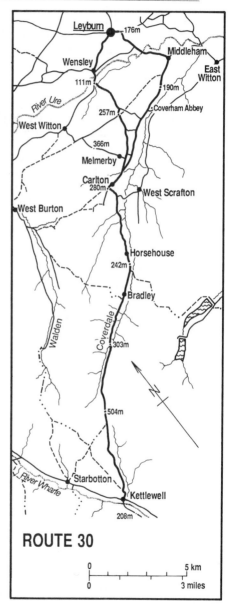

ROUTE 30

0 _____ 5 km
0 _____ 3 miles

the road is more down than up to **Horsehouse**. This hamlet, situated where the valley is crossed by tracks from Nidderdale and Walden, earned its name through being the place where the packhorses of yore were 'fed'. Cyclists can do likewise as here are the last inn and shop before Kettlewell. The way from Nidderdale via Dead Man's Hill, a useful through route for cyclists, is described in Route 10.

The road continues its up-and-down course through Woodale and **Bradley** before dropping to the infant River Cover. There follows a stiff ascent out of the head of the valley, the road passing the Hunter Stone, an ancient waymarker. The one building in sight is an old shooting lodge, stranded in the middle of the moor. This could once claim to be the highest inhabited house in Yorkshire. The descent at first is gradual, but at the end of this is the longest and worst pitch of the descent — **Park Rash**, which falls at 1 in 4. Near the foot of Park Rash a stile on the left indicates the path to Dow Cave, about a 10-minute walk from the road. The road runs down a narrow side valley with a good forward view down Wharfedale to Kilnsey Crag and beyond. At the end of this side valley the second steep stage of the descent brings the rider into the village of Kettlewell.

For **Kettlewell** and the roads up and down Wharfedale and Littondale see Route 4. If heading direct to Grassington ($6^1/_4$ miles) the minor road down the east of the valley via Conistone will be found a delight, and a rest-cure after the trials of Coverdale. Across the valley the overhanging cliff of Kilnsey Crag is prominent. For Grassington and Wharfedale below that town see Route 1.

ROUTE 31
LEYBURN to REETH (SWALEDALE) and BARNARD CASTLE

Distances from Leyburn (miles): **Bellerby** $1^3/_4$, **Halfpenny House** $3^1/_2$, **Reeth** $10^1/_4$ (direct 8). For distances beyond Reeth see below.

INTRODUCTION

This is really two routes joined together — from Leyburn to Reeth and from Reeth to Barnard Castle, as no one would wish to make so brief an acquaintance with Swaledale.

The A6108 is by far the easiest link between Wensleydale and Swaledale, as all crossings further west involve substantially more hillclimbing. The direct road from Leyburn to Reeth has little to commend it: there are long uphill stretches first passing quarries and then military training ranges. The only noteworthy views commence with the long descent to Swaledale, on which care is required in places. The main advantage of this direct road is to those heading for Grinton Lodge Youth Hostel, passed on the way, which otherwise involves quite a push up from the main road in the valley.

North of Reeth the usual road to Barnard Castle traverses the remote upland area known as the Stang, and the best scenery is in the all-too-briefly visited valleys of the Arkle Beck and the Greta. Although a quiet road it is an ancient one (used by the Romans) and at its busiest when the Arkengarthdale leadmines were active. Also covered is an easterly alternative, via Newsham, more as an introduction to the remote area north-east of Reeth than as a through route.

THE ROUTE

The exit from Wensleydale to beyond Bellerby is across uninteresting upland, and not until on the Swaledale side does the scenery pick up.

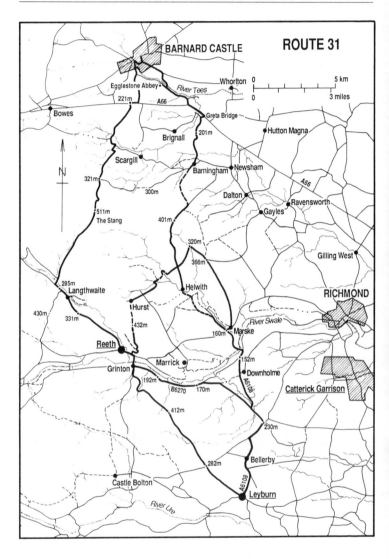

The minor road to Reeth leaves the A6108 just west of **Walburn Hall**, which retains some sixteenth-century architectural features.

By keeping to the A6108 and crossing the Swale at Downholme Bridge the alternative route given below, from Reeth to Barnard Castle via Newsham, can be reached, via either Helwith or Marske Moor, as described in Route 27. Leyburn to Marske is 8 miles.

The road forward increases in beauty as it nears the Swale Gorge. Across the valley of the Gill Beck old lynchets — hillside terraces for cultivation — are very noticeable near **Downholme**. The main road up Swaledale is reached near the fourth milestone from Reeth. This onward section is easy and fully described in Route 26. First the isolated tower of Ellerton Priory is seen on the right then, a little further, Marrick Priory comes into view just across the river. **Grinton** has an ancient church and was formerly more important than the upstart mining village of **Reeth**.

Reeth to Barnard Castle via Newsham
Distance from Reeth (miles): **Hurst** $2^3/_4$, **Holgate Crossroads** 5, **Newsham** 10, **Barnard Castle** 17.

This route is chiefly of appeal to cyclists through its use of an old road, in parts now just a track, which led from Reeth to Ravensworth and the port of Stockton. The initial rise out of Swaledale over Fremington Edge is 250m after which it is a series of ups and downs over generally uninteresting moorland.

A quarter of a mile east of Reeth a turning (no signpost) winds up through Fremington, continuing as a narrow lane slanting up the valley side. It is tarred most of the way, finally becoming a well made cart track. This separates into several strands on nearing the summit, but a gate in the the ridgetop wall indicates the way forward. Beyond the gate the track is in extremely good condition, running due north to the old leadmining community of **Hurst**. The mines were being worked in Roman times and were most active in the nineteenth century before the sudden and disastrous slump of the 1880s. The hamlet is just a shadow of its former size and there is no longer an inn. The tarred road leading down to **Marrick** is entered through a metal gate: southbound, the only key to this being the way to Reeth is the old rectangular chimney almost alongside the track.

Following the road downhill, keep straight on at the next crossroads and a mile further straight on at a sign 'Unsuitable for Motors'. This becomes a gated track which drops to a ford and footbridge on Holgate

Beck and after a steep climb up the opposite bank becomes a tarred road again. Indeed at the lonely Holgate crossroads, a little further on, there is (or was) a roadsign directing back to Hurst! At this crossroads the road straight on is that up from **Marske** (5 miles), though a more interesting way is via **Helwith**, as described in Route 27.

Turning north again, the road rises to a height of about 400m as it winds over Holgate Moor, culminating in a long straight descent to **Newsham**. If aiming for Barnard Castle a side track, starting about $\frac{1}{4}$ mile past the last summit, can be taken down to Barningham, though no time will be saved. Keep to the regular road — you have deserved it!

Newsham lies on a pleasant minor road linking Richmond (8 miles) with **Barnard Castle** (7 miles), the continuation of which is described in Route 33. With a good map one can pick out useful minor roads north to Bishop Auckland (17 miles) or east to Darlington (15 miles).

Reeth to Barnard Castle via The Stang
Distances from Reeth (miles): **Langthwaite** $3\frac{1}{4}$, **The Stang** (summit) $6\frac{1}{4}$, **A66 junction** $11\frac{1}{2}$ (Bowes $14\frac{3}{4}$), **Barnard Castle** 14.

The journey up Arkengarthdale is hard going, as the road runs some way above and away from the river. The descent to Langthwaite provides some welcome relief and an improvement in the scenery. For notes on the vicinity see Route 28.

Just beyond Langthwaite a road comes in from Feetham, across the hill in Swaledale. This is tough going and inferior to the longer way round via Reeth.

Half a mile beyond Langthwaite the Barnard Castle road crosses the Arkle Beck and from the bridge rises abruptly, an ascent of 130m, to a brow from where the road onwards to the Stang is revealed — a most disheartening view. When eventually the distant summit is reached, at the boundary of North Yorkshire and Durham, the prospect north is scarcely better, extending over the featureless moors west of the Tees.

The descent through **Stang Forest** includes a very steep zig-zag but otherwise provides fast and easy cycling. The going is not all downhill, however, as a bleak upland plateau is traversed before the road drops to the valleys first of the Greta and then of the Tees.

There are some interesting side turnings from the Barnard Castle road. The first, at the former Hill Top Inn, is signposted Hope, but actually continues to Barningham. About half a mile is untarred, but overall it is a reasonable cycling route. Further north there is a turning for Scargill and Barningham,

Langthwaite, Arkengarthdale

a very pleasant road, and at Rutherford a route, part bridleway, heads off to
Bowes. All these side excursions are covered in Route 33.

Beyond the Hope turn, there is an unexpected sting in the form of a
1 in 6 hill up. At the foot of the succeeding straight take care, as there
is a very sharp left bend. On reaching the main A66 this is followed
eastwards only a short distance before turning off again for Barnard
Castle. This is mostly downhill and from the hilltop above Stratforth
there is a good view of the castle itself, towering over the river. Once
across the Tees there is a long climb up to the town centre. For **Barnard
Castle** see Route 33.

ROUTE 32
KIRKBY STEPHEN to BROUGH
and BARNARD CASTLE

Distances from Kirkby Stephen (miles): **Brough** $4^1/_4$, **North Stain-more** $6^1/_2$, **Rey Cross** (summit) 11 ($9^1/_2$ via Barras), **Bowes** $17^1/_4$, **Barnard Castle** 22.

INTRODUCTION

The A66, the main route from eastern England to Scotland, is one which should be shunned by cyclists if at all possible. Not only is it one of little scenic interest, but the constant stream of traffic, much of it heavy lorries, makes it an unpleasant one for the rider. It should certainly not be considered westbound, as the uphill plod from Bowes, probably into a headwind and on a road barely wide enough for heavy traffic to pass, is potentially dangerous. There are proposals to dual most of the unimproved sections of this road. On the Cumbria side some of the road has already been widened or dualled so in general the traffic is less obtrusive. In any case from Kirkby Stephen much of the upward toil can be made on minor roads via Winton and Barras, which join the A66 about 2 miles west of the summit (attempts to cut this last corner will not save time). While this route has its merits eastbound, coming west the steadier gradients via Brough will be found too good to miss.

The Stainmore Gap, despite being such a bleak moorland crossing, is the lowest point at which the Pennine chain can be crossed for many miles north or south. It was utilised by the Romans for one of their highways which is closely followed by the present A66. Overall there is a rise of 270m from Brough, 310m from the Tees at Barnard Castle.

THE ROUTE

The A685 provides an easy run north from **Kirkby Stephen**, the only

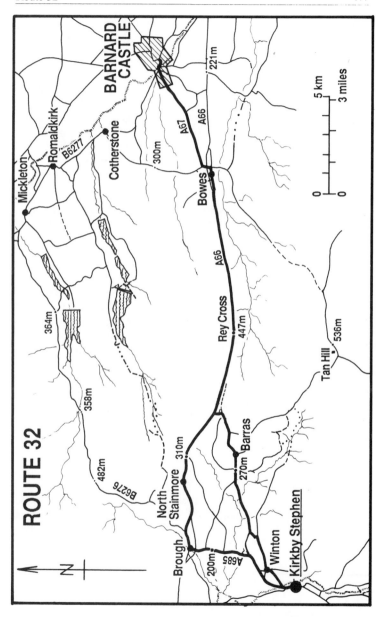

hill coming just before Church Brough. Brough Castle stands on a prominent knoll which was the site of an earlier Roman fort. Most of the keep of the Norman castle survives, despite a most turbulent history.

Brough to Middleton-in-Teesdale is $14^1/_4$ miles. If you are obliged to cross the Pennines to Barnard Castle there is a lot for making virtue out of necessity and seeing some Teesdale scenery en route. This link (B6276) itself is a very quiet road over lonely moors. There is a long but steady climb from Brough to the summit (482m), followed by a drop to Grains o' th' Beck, the halfway point. Thereafter the road, rather a dull one, maintains its height to Thringarth before finally descending into Teesdale.

Brough lies along what was until recently the main A66 but now its principal street is practically deserted. Villages such as Brough and Bowes which relied on passing custom to sustain local facilities have suffered commercially from the removal of traffic, however desirable that may have been from the environmental point of view. Turning right at the clocktower the old road climbs for a mile or so to join the bypass, whereafter the long ascent continues through North Stainmore to culminate in 2 miles of dual carriageway. Approaching the summit the old railway comes alongside, once the second-highest passenger line in England. It is hard to believe that at the end of the last century the railway had deprived the road of its traffic to the extent that grass grew over it. Now the situation is reversed. A little beyond the county boundary is the actual summit, 447m. On the south side of the road is **Rey Cross**, a humble and time worn stone marking the ancient boundary between the kingdoms of Northumbria and Strathclyde. The cross and this section of road lie within the site of a Roman camp, the northern and eastern outlines of which can still be traced, though the spot is bleak and hardly conducive to such exploration. Featureless moorland stretches in all directions.

The descent on the east side is steady, the road keeping to the straight Roman alignment. On the skyline to the south is the Tan Hill Inn. A little before Bowes an obvious gate on the right leads into the old road through the village.

Bowes, like Brough, now slumbers, for most travellers counting no more than just another signpost off the A66. It is however a place of some past importance, as it was a Roman station at the junction of two roads. Later the site was adopted for a Norman castle, the keep of which, shorn of any internal features, still stands guard over the village. Bowes and the surrounding area was the home of a number of harshly-run schools of a type pilloried so successfully by Dickens in *Nicholas Nickleby*.

The Brough to Middleton road in winter

Some distances from Bowes (miles): **Cotherstone** 5, **Greta Bridge** 6, **Scotch Corner** $15^1/_2$, **Richmond** $17^3/_4$ (Route 30), **Reeth** $14^3/_4$ (Route 31), **Tan Hill** $8^3/_4$.

The continuation by the A66 to Greta Bridge is more of the same — tedious straights and heavy traffic, though mostly downhill. The few extra miles via Barnard Castle are worth it. For the southern alternative, via Scargill to Newsham etc, see Route 33.

From Bowes the Barnard Castle road (A67) is quieter with much fewer heavy vehicles. It crosses a dull tableland which obligingly slopes more and more downhill as it nears the Tees (coming west this provides a most dreary plod for a good 2 miles). There remains then only the climb up the winding main street into **Barnard Castle**, for which see Route 33.

ROUTE 33
RICHMOND to BARNARD CASTLE

Distances from Richmond (miles): **Kirby Hill** 4³/₄, **Newsham** 8, **Barningham** 9¹/₂, **Greta Bridge** 11³/₄ (Bowes 17³/₄), **Abbey Bridge** 13¹/₂, **Barnard Castle** 15¹/₄.

INTRODUCTION

While motorists will seek to maximise their use of the A66 between these two attractive towns, wise cyclists will avoid it as far as possible. Not only is it a busy traffic route but also a monotonous series of undulating straights. The route described keeps mostly to quiet back-roads, but even so the A66 has to be followed a little if excessive deviations are not to be made.

THE ROUTE

For **Richmond** see Route 26. Heading east from the town centre, the road (signposted Ravensworth) turns up at the traffic lights and climbs steeply, attaining a height of 210m. Thereafter the road follows an undulating course through pleasant countryside. Four miles from Richmond turn left to continue via Kirby Hill, on a road overlooking a broad valley. Below lies the village of **Ravensworth**, where a lone tower is almost all that survives of a once-extensive castle.

    Kirby Hill consists of some old houses and the church arranged round a pleasant village green, the whole lying just off the through road. This is a very appealing cycling route, winding through Gayles and Dalton to **Newsham**, where a decision must be taken on which route to proceed by.

    If desirous of avoiding the A66 completely, then the admittedly roundabout route via Hutton and Whorlton may be recommended. These are very quiet roads, and apart from the dip to cross the Tees at Whorlton very easy. There

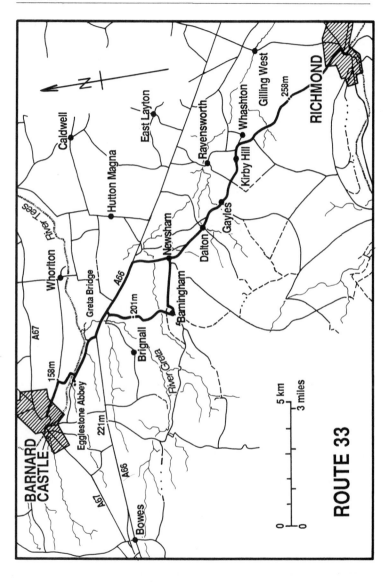

ROUTE 33

is some fine riverside scenery at Whorlton, which may be reached from the bridge by path or by a bridleway from the top of the village. Newsham to Whorlton is $5^1/_4$ miles, Barnard Castle 9 miles.

The most direct route from Newsham to Barnard Castle leads forward to the A66 and requires that road to be followed for about 2 miles to the turning for Egglestone Abbey and Barnard Castle. The alternative, looping round via Barningham, increases the total distance only slightly, but involves more hillclimbing.

Newsham to Bowes (9 miles), via Barningham and Scargill, is an interesting and varied alternative to slogging up the A66. The road rises to Barningham, a pleasant village, beyond which it runs through richly green scenery, near the deep valley of the Greta. Scargill Castle, prominently named on some maps, consists of a few scant remains now forming a farm outbuilding. On reaching the Barnard Castle road this is followed north for a few hundred metres, to Rutherford, where the track at the side of the farm leads up to the moor. Where this ceases a grassy track (bridleway) carries onwards, following the wall, but in parts the cycle will have to be wheeled which is easy. In a mile or so the end of an enclosed track, long visible ahead, is reached, and this soon becomes a tarred road down to Bowes.

Those aiming for Arkengarthdale, via The Stang, can cut the corner beyond Barningham by a minor road to Hope. This starts off tarred, continuing beyond Haythwaite as a metalled road. After crossing a deep gill turn left, the tarred surface resuming in half a mile. Watch out for some steep hills beyond.

For those heading for Barnard Castle the A66 must be employed to cross the **Greta Bridge,** the parallel old bridge of 1789 now only leading to Brignall. Probably not one in a hundred motorists who speed across the river realises that, Greta Bridge and its surroundings are rich in historic and literary connections. Sir Walter Scott visited the area on various occasions and here wrote the *Rokeby Sonnets*. For the cyclist the pick of the scenery is reached from the Barnard Castle road, which turns out of the A66 a little way up the hill beyong Greta Bridge and skirts Rokeby Park.

At a bend a private road (public footpath) follows the Tees downstream to where it is joined by the tumbling waters of the Greta. This is a lovely spot. Higher up the Greta can be crossed by the Dairy Bridge (good views up and down stream). The road continues to Mortham Tower. This is a very interesting building, showing its development from a fourteenth-century castellated peel tower to a post medieval country house. The house is private, but passed by the public footpath, which leads back to Greta Bridge.

Returning to the Barnard Castle road, in a mile or so **Abbey Bridge** is reached, an elaborate structure with a single span high above the Tees. Before crossing it, carry on along the side road to **Egglestone Abbey**. Relatively little of the abbey, founded in 1189, remains, but the site is a pretty one, overlooking the Tees, and well worth the detour. Returning to Abbey Bridge, the road rises at first and then provides an easy run into Barnard Castle, with the Bowes Museum passed on the way.

Visitors who have thought Richmond unique will be equally pleased by **Barnard Castle**. Its winding main street, in which is the octagonal market house, provides a good selection of shops, but turns its back on the castle. Approaching the town from the west, however, the keep cannot be missed, as it still stands guard over the Tees Bridge. The castle dates from the Norman settlement of the north in the wake of the Conquest.

The town has another claim on the tourist, the Bowes Museum. Housed in a handsome *château*-style building (it was originally intended for a site in France) it was planned from the outset to be a public museum of continental art. As well as a great many paintings it includes china, sculpture, furniture, many other valuable collections and items of more local interest.

Some distances from Barnard Castle (miles): **Middleton-in-Teesdale** $10^1/_2$ (Route 34) , **Brough** 18 (Route 32), **Reeth** 14 (Route 31), **Scotch Corner** $14^1/_2$, **Darlington** 16, **Bishop Auckland** $14^1/_2$, **Durham** $24^1/_2$, **Stanhope** 18.

Egglestone Abbey

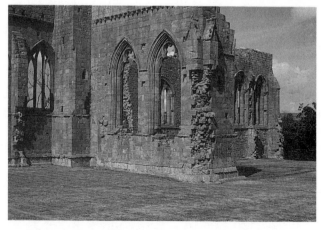

ROUTE 34
BARNARD CASTLE to UPPER TEESDALE

Distances from Barnard Castle (miles): **Lartington** $2^3/_4$, **Cother-stone** $4^1/_4$, **Romaldkirk** $6^1/_4$, **Mickleton** $8^1/_4$, **Middleton-in-Teesdale** $10^1/_2$, **Newbiggin** 13, **High Force Hotel** 15, **Langdon Beck Hotel** $17^3/_4$, **county boundary** 24, **Alston** $32^1/_2$.

INTRODUCTION

The inclusion of Teesdale in a book on the Yorkshire Dales may seem to be stretching geography a little, but until 1974 the Tees as far north as Caldron Snout formed the boundary between the then North Riding and the county of Durham. Scenically, as well, it can hold its own with the finest Dales' country. 'Tourist' Teesdale is generally considered to begin at the meeting of the Tees and Greta, south of Barnard Castle, and culminate in the magnificent surroundings of High Force, a run of about 20 miles. This scenic interest mainly arises from the presence of the Whin Sill, that basalt shelf which is exposed in the bed of the Tees at the waterfalls of High Force and elsewhere. The Tees itself is heavily peat-stained, which rather detracts from its appeal. There are many miles of pretty riverside which are only accessible to the active pedestrian, but the cyclist who is prepared to break his or her journey will find plenty to linger over. For the rider, as opposed to the walker, Teesdale really begins among the gentle byways that follow the river on its lower stages, from Darlington to Barnard Castle, through a succession of pretty villages.

This chapter is concerned with Teesdale above Barnard Castle, covering the valley road to Langdon Beck, then briefly the moorland road to Alston and the famous watershed crossing via High Cup to Dufton and Appleby. If returning to Barnard Castle then High Force is the obvious place to turn round, as beyond anything must be an anti-climax.

THE ROUTE

For **Barnard Castle** see Route 33. Of the two roads from Barnard Castle to Middleton, that on the western (formerly Yorkshire) side of the river is greatly to be preferred. The B6278 is a moorland road of very little interest before Eggleston. From the old Tees Bridge below the town and castle, the B6277 rises steadily to **Lartington**, a neat estate village. There is a long descent to **Cotherstone**, another quaint place, once famous for cheeses. Opposite the Hare and Hounds a narrow lane drops to some pleasant riverside scenery where the Balder meets the Tees. On a knoll above is the site of a small castle, of which nothing now remains.

Running west from Cotherstone, Baldersdale, a side-valley, makes a worthwhile digression, though the roads are far from easy. The valley can be crossed along or just below the Balderhead Reservoir dam (7 miles), near which is the Baldersdale Youth Hostel. Above this top dam the valley is much barer and further exploration is not worthwhile. A bridleway runs west from Balderhead to North Stainmore ($2^1/_2$ hours) near Brough, but this is not all defined and very exposed. From Baldersdale the ridge can be crossed into Lunedale, but it is better to keep to the north side of the former, via Hury, so rejoining the main route at Romaldkirk.

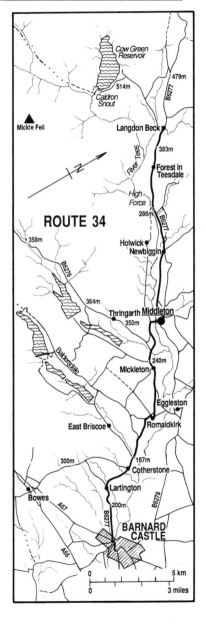

The next village in Teesdale, **Romaldkirk**, is another picture postcard, which you will have to turn aside from the main road to appreciate. Its well-proportioned church dates from the twelfth and thirteenth centuries.

A mile north of Romaldkirk is Eggleston Bridge, one of the finest on the Tees. Middleton may then be reached along the north side of the river, the road running high above the valley floor and offering good views.

Keeping to the west bank of the river the road next passes through Mickleton, then dips to cross the Lune below the disused railway viaduct. A few more ups and downs bring one to Middleton.

The only place of any size between Barnard Castle and Alston is **Middleton**, a straggling town which was formerly a centre of the leadmining industry. Its current populaton of 1,200 is half what it was 100 years ago. It is now kept alive by tourism and provides plenty of accommodation and refreshment. The church has a rare detached belfry.

Some distances from Middleton (miles): **Brough** $14^1/_4$, **Stanhope** 13, **Bishop Auckland** 21.

Middleton-in-Teesdale to Brough ($14^1/_4$ miles) is a quiet and lonely road with no intermediate point of interest or refreshment. Most of the climbing is done in the first 2 or 3 miles from Middleton, to Thringarth, a hamlet vying with Greenhow for the bleakest situation in the north. Thereafter the road takes an up and down course along the side of a broad and featureless valley, which even the presence of the Selset Reservoir does little to relieve. The road dips to cross the Lune at Grains o' th' Beck, the halfway point, whereafter it climbs again to its summit, 482m a little beyond the county boundary between Durham and Cumbria. There are good views of the western escarpments of the Pennines, the Howgill Fells and the distant hills of Lakeland on the 4-mile descent to Brough (Route 32).

Beyond Middleton the road is an easy one, rising only slowly in keeping with the valley. The river runs nearby for almost the only time in its long course, and the scenery is pleasant. Just past Newbiggin, and reached by a little loop road, is the **Bowlees Visitor Centre**. Housed in a former chapel, it includes exhibits of Teesdale flora and fauna. Nearby is a picnicking area in a pretty gorge, which contains a number of waterfalls. Across the B6277 from Bowlees a footpath leads down to **Winch Bridge** on the Tees. Hereabouts is some of the best riverside scenery in Teesdale and a stroll up or down river makes a pleasant interlude. Just upstream is Low Force, a series of cascades.

On the far side of the valley is a minor road from Middleton to Holwick (3 miles). Beyond Holwick it continues as a cart track (footpath only) to Holwick Head House. Here a much more awkward path leads up the south side of the Tees to High Force. The river cannot be crossed near the fall, but there is a private footbridge below Holwick Head which walkers may use.

Continuing on the B6277 a short run brings one to the High Force Hotel, opposite which a toll-path leads down to **High Force.** This, the mightiest fall in England, is a sight never to be forgotten. The Tees thunders over a step in the Whin Sill to drop 22m to the deep pools beneath.

Apart from **Caldron Snout** the best of Teesdale now lies behind. The B6277 turns away from the river, and out of Teesdale proper, and climbs through woods to emerge on the edge of a wild moorland basin, a series of knolls and scattered white-painted farms. On the right is the little post office and shop of **Forest in Teesdale** and half a mile further the **Langdon Beck** Youth Hostel.

Langdon Beck to Caldron Snout by footpath is a considerable walk but given the total lack of interest in the approach via Cow Green may be suggested to those with time available. It is $3^1/_2$ miles each way, and allow 3 hours. The track starting opposite the Youth Hostel leads down to bridge the Harwood Beck, after which it joins the Pennine Way (all well marked). In a further mile, at Widdybank, it enters the impressive gorge of the Tees, which it follows for the remainder of the way. Return as you came.

Caldron Snout is a cascade rather than a fall, the water tumbling down a steep bed of doleritic rocks. Starting at the bottom you escape being reminded that what you see is merely the overflow from the reservoir.

Langdon Beck to Alston
This is an excellently engineered road, courtesy of the Alston leadmining interests. As Langdon Beck is about 400m in elevation even the road's summit level of 598m is relatively easily attained, unless you are on the receiving end of a headwind. Ahead is Cross Fell, highest point in the Pennines, and its disfigured neighbour, Great Dun Fell. The South Tyne Valley provides a triumphant descent to Alston.

Langdon Beck to Cow Green, High Cup and Dufton
Distances from Langdon Beck Hotel (miles): **Caldron Snout** 4, **High Cup** 9, **Dufton** 13. Allow 3 to $3^1/_2$ hours.

This was a famous rough-stuff cycling route long before it became part of the Pennine Way or Maize Beck was bridged. There are no physical difficulties preventing a bicycle from being taken across, but the going is very wet in places and the terrain exposed and remote.

The side turning at the hotel climbs steadily for over 2 miles before descending to the shores of the **Cow Green Reservoir**. Its construction was a very controversial issue as Upper Teesdale is the last home of a number of rare plants. As a scenic attraction its value is nil. From the summit of the road, near some mine workings, a gated side-road runs down to a bridge just below the dam. This is just above Caldron Snout, and a footpath can be taken beside the stream as it tumbles down to the main valley floor.

At the bridge the tarred road ends, a metalled lane continuing to the lonely farm of Birkdale. The route continues straight on as a well trodden path, initially over peaty moorland, and passing some old mine workings. A long descent brings one alongside **Maize Beck** and presently a signpost is reached. This indicates the alternative route, bridging the stream a mile higher up, but if at all possible the beck should be forded as there is then some surprisingly good cycling to be found almost all the way to **High Cup**. This is one of the most impressive scenes in Britain, an enormous scooped-out hollow, lined with basalt cliffs, with the Lakeland peaks seen far away across the Vale of Eden. The path contours awkwardly around the rocky rim of the valley for some way before dropping to meet a cart track leading down to **Dufton**. Anywhere offering refreshment and a bed for the night would be welcome after this crossing, but Dufton is an especially neat and handsome village, with shop, Youth Hostel and pub. Dufton to Penrith is 13 miles, to Appleby $4^1/_2$ miles.

And what better way to end a cycling tour, than to return south from Appleby over the Settle and Carlisle railway, looking down from its mighty viaducts onto the narrow winding ribbons of roads, scenes of past toils and triumphs while cycling in the Yorkshire Dales.

USEFUL INFORMATION FOR CYCLISTS

Cycle Dealers and Cycle Hirers

This list covers the parts of Yorkshire, Cumbria and Durham included in the book, but for reasons of space the numerous dealers in the larger towns and cities surrounding have been omitted. While it is hoped that the list is as comprehensive as possible changes are always occuring so confirmation by telephone is advisable. Please note that, although certain shops will undertake repairs, work may not be able to be handled immediately. Where advertised, cycle hire is usually available at daily or weekly rates. A deposit and proof of identity is invariably required. A prior call is wise to ensure that bikes of the right number and type are available.

Appleby
Appleby Cycle Centre
J & C Harrison
☎ (07863) 51870
From the station pass through yard alongside railway to far end of track. Cycle hire available all year round.

Aysgarth, Wensleydale
See Thoralby

Barnard Castle
The Toy Shop
11 The Bank (lower main street)
Cycle parts and accessories.

Bedale
G. Dawkins

Bridge Garage, 36 Emgate
☎ (0677) 22491
Cycle parts, accessories and repairs.
Cycle hire available all year round.

Catterick
Mountain Bike Dales Tours
See Reeth

Dent
The North Country Shop
The Filling Station, Dent
☎ (05875) 460
Mountain bike hire.

Grassington
Cobblestones Café, The Square
☎ (0756) 752303
Cycle hire.

Harrogate
Ace Cycles
139 Kings Road
☎ (0423) 508417
Follow road past Conference Centre
towards Bilton.
Cycle parts, accessories and repairs.
Cycle hire (including mountain
bikes) available most of year.
Closed Wednesday.

H. Acklam
11 Bower Road
☎ (0423) 65125
400m north of railway station.
Cycle parts, accessories and repairs.

Baines Bros
Station Parade
☎ (0423) 66001
300m north of railway station.
Cycle parts, accessories and repairs.

John Donoghue Cycles
41-43 High Street
Starbeck
☎ (0423) 883184
Cycle parts, accessories and repairs.
Cycle hire (including mountain
bikes) available all year round.

Harrogate Cycle Centre
55 Knaresborough Road
☎ (0423) 885196
Cycle parts, accessories and repairs.

Spa Cycles
1 Wedderburn Road
(off Wetherby Road)
☎ (0423) 887003
Cycle parts, accessories and repairs.
Cycle hire (including mountain
bikes) based at Pateley Bridge.
Available all year round.

G. W. Johnson Cycles
5 Cheltenham Parade
Between Royal Hall and station.
☎ (0423) 569251
Cycle parts, accessories and repairs.
Early closing Wednesday.

Horsehouse, Coverdale
Thwaite Arms
Horsehouse
☎ (0969) 40206
Mid-way between Kettlewell and
Leyburn. Mountain bike hire
available all year round.

Ilkley
Wharfedale Cycle Depot
32 Leeds Road
☎ (0943) 607957
Cycle parts, accessories and repairs.

Keld, Upper Swaledale
Keld Bike Centre
Keld Lodge Youth Hostel
☎ (0748) 86259
Cycle parts, accessories and repairs.
Cycle hire (including mountain
bikes) available all year round.
Accompanied daily and weekend
tours by arrangement.

Kettlewell, Wharfedale
W & R. M. Wilkinson
The Garage
Kettlewell
☎ (075676) 225
Cycle parts and cycle hire (includ-
ing mountain bikes) available from
April to October.

Kirkby Stephen
H. S. Robinson

2 Market Street
☎ (07683) 71519
Cycle parts, accessories and repairs.
Cycle hire (including mountain
bikes) available all year round.
Early closing, Thursday.

Knaresborough
Thompson Cycle Sport
2 Cheapside
☎ (0423) 864970
Cycle parts, accessories and repairs.
Closed Thursday.

Otley
Chevin Cycles
34 Gay Lane (Leeds Road)
☎ (0943) 462773
Cycle parts, accessories and repairs.
Closed Wednesday.

Pateley Bridge
Cycloan
Riverside
☎ (0423) 711981 or 711383
Mountain bike hire.

Spa Cycles
Mount Pleasant Farm
See under Harrogate.
Cycle hire.

Reeth, Swaledale
Mountain Bike Dales Tours
11 Rowan Court
Catterick Village
N. Yorks
DL10 7RS
☎ (0748) 811885
Organised weekend and day
mountain bike tours at Reeth. Bikes
provided or bring your own.

Richmond
Arthur Caygill Cycles
Borough Road, Gallowfields
Trading Estate (north of town
centre) also at Saturday Indoor
Market, Richmond
☎ (0748) 5469
Cycle parts, accessories and repairs.
Cycle hire (including mountain
bikes) all year round.

Ripon
John Donoghue
The Cycle Centre
Westgate
☎ (0765) 701395
Cycle parts, accessories and repairs.
Cycle hire (including mountain
bikes) available all year round.

Settle
Settle Cycles
Duke Street (main road)
☎ (0729) 22216
Cycle parts, accessories and repairs.
Cycle hire (including mountain
bikes) available all year.

Skipton
Bike Hogan
3 Water Street (road to Gargrave)
☎ (0756) 4386
Cycle parts, accessories and repairs.
Mountain bike hire available all
year round. Closed Tuesday.

Northern Auto Supplies
25 Water Street
☎ (0756) 4363
Cycle parts and accessories.

Thoralby
Sadler Cycle Hire
The Post Office
Thoralby
☎ (0969) 663205
Cyele hire (including mountain
bikes) available all year round.
Early closing Thursday.

Cyclists' Touring Club
A national association devoted to the
encouragement of cycling and the
protection of cyclists' interests.
Membership includes third party in-
surance and the club runs a legal aid
scheme for members involved in road
accidents. The touring department
offers a wide ranging information
service. Local rides and events are
arranged by the various district asso-
ciations throughout the country. For
membership enquiries write and enclose an sae to:

CTC National Headquarters
Cotterell House
69 Meadrow
Godalming
Surrey
GU7 3HS
☎ (04868) 7217

National Park Information Centres
Aysgarth Falls
On road to Carperby
☎ (0969) 663424

Clapham
☎ (04685) 419

Grassington
Hebden Road
☎ (0756) 752748

Hawes
Old Station Car Park
☎ (0969) 667450

Malham
☎ (07293) 363

Sedbergh
Main Street
☎ (05396) 20125

Weather information can be obtained
from the centres, or by phoning
Weatherline (0898) 500417, covering
the Yorkshire Dales. A more local
forecast, daily in August and at weekends throughout the year, is available
on Dent (05875) 462.

Rough Stuff Fellowship
Those interested in exploring Brit-
ain's network of bridleways and old
tracks may wish to join the Rough
Stuff Fellowship.
For details send an sae to:
New Membership Secretary
A.J. Mathews
9 Liverpool Avenue
Ainsdale
Southport
Merseyside
PR8 3NE

Youth Hostels
For membership enquiries write and
enclose an sae to:
YHA Trevelyan House
8 St Stephens Hill
St Albans
Herts
AL1 2DY